Hit and Run!:

How To Beat Blackjack As A Way Of Life

HIT & RUN!

♠

How to Beat Blackjack As A Way Of Life

by

ARNOLD BRUCE LEVY
INTRODUCTION BY LYLE STUART

Barricade Books ♦ New York, NY

Published by Barricade Books Inc.
185 Bridge Plaza North, Suite 308A
Fort Lee, NJ 07024

Library of Congress Cataloging-in-Publication Data
Levy, Arnold Bruce.
    Hit and run : how to beat blackjack as a way of life / by
    Arnold Bruce Levy ; introduction by Lyle Stuart.
        p. cm.
    ISBN: 1-56980-140-1 (alk. paper)
    1. Blackjack (Game) 2. Gambling. I. Title.

    GV1295.B55 L48 2000
    795.4'23--dc21   00-041381

Printed in the United States of America.
First printing

Dedicated to The Champ

Wise Mentor, Faithful Friend—
A Winner, Both in the Casinos and in Life.

Contents

♠

Contents

♠

Publisher's Introduction

Blackjack is the most popular game in the casino. Dollar-for-dollar, it isn't my favorite game. As I wrote in my books, *Lyle Stuart on Baccarat* and *Winning at Casino Gambling*, both craps and baccarat give the player better odds for his money. Blackjack for me is just the occasional fling, a hit-and-run foray during a casino trip.

Yes, there have been expert blackjack players—Thorp, Lawrence Revere, Richard Canfield, to name a few. All have one thing in common: They're expert card-counters. I am not. However, you don't need the memory of an elephant or the logic of an Einstein to win at blackjack. In *Winning at Casino Gambling* I told of Arnold Levy, a friend who is associated with me in my book publishing company. Arnold couldn't count cards in a blackjack game to save his butt. But, more often than not, Arnold does beat blackjack.

Arnold Bruce Levy is a player who as a rule does well in Atlantic City because he has a plan and follows it. He always travels there by bus. He carries with him a 3 x 5 card to record what happens at each casino. His "score card," as he refers to it, also acts to rein him in.

First, he writes down the name of the casino he is about to enter. Then, next to the name, he writes a modest number—maybe $200 or $300. That's his goal. He usually plays until he reaches the goal he set down for himself on the card, and then he exits and hastens over to the next casino.

I have known him to play in all twelve casinos in Atlantic City within ten hours. Sure, he has his ups and downs—no one can win every time—but more often than not, he comes away a winner.

Sometimes it's just a few hundred dollars. Sometimes it's thousands.

Arnold never asks for credit from the casinos and he never writes checks. The result is that, at most, all he can lose is the cash in his pocket, which he carefully limits. Yes, there have been times that the casinos have cleaned him out. Yet even on those occasions he has thanked his lucky stars that he had his return bus ticket tucked away safely in his wallet.

This is one man whose years of casino experience have made him so goal-oriented that he is able to hit and run successfully. Some months ago, Arnold accomplished a rather spectacular feat. Not only did he gamble in all twelve Atlantic City casinos that day, but he won money in every single one of them. In fact, he returned to two of the casinos before boarding the bus to New York, and won money a *second* time in each! The Bottom Line: fourteen forays, fourteen blackjack tables, fourteen casinos, fourteen winning sessions.

I was impressed.

Then, three weeks later, Arnold arrived at our offices all smiles. He passed around his "score card" from his previous day "at the seashore," as he put it. Nine hours, fourteen winning forays at the blackjack tables. Again, no losses anywhere.

"I hit and ran, and I beat blackjack—again," Arnold chortled proudly.

"That's it!" I interjected. *"Hit and Run*—a great title. Now go ahead and write a book and tell us how you did it."

Lyle Stuart
Stuyvesant, New York
August, 2000

Preface
The "Experts" and Their "Expertise"

These days it seems that anybody who has made more than two trips to a casino has written a book on how to win. I'm willing to bet there is more than one gambling book out there written by an idiot who never even saw the inside of a casino. One pundit with a hardcover book on wagering, bearing the imprint of a major publisher, writes about betting at the Sands in Las Vegas with $50 chips. Maybe this asshole ducked into the Sands to use the Men's Room, but I guarantee he didn't stay long enough to look at the chips on the tables. No $50 denomination chips exist or ever existed in any Vegas casino. Not ever.

Mark Twain once quipped, "It isn't what people *don't* know that'll hurt them, it's what they *do* know that just ain't so."

Another "expert," writing on how to beat the slot machines, gives the reader a hot tip: Always play the slots on the aisle, as these are the ones the casino have set to be loose so the passersby will be seduced into playing because it looks so easy to win. The only thing wrong with this "inside tip" is that it's false. *All* the slots in *all* the casinos are blindly computer-controlled with respect to the winning combinations, so one slot machine is as good or as bad as the next. And I've read in more than one gambling book written by a self-anointed "expert" that the machines at the top, or end, of the aisle are the ones that pay off best. Total applesauce. The machines in between are just as likely to pay off as the ones at either end.

Another so-called expert, this one on blackjack, advises the reader with great authority to *always* take insurance, and to take advantage of "surrender" when offered. In reality, both are piss-poor moves for a player. Still another self-styled expert on playing the craps table gave in his book the odds on Place and Come bets on the numbers, except he gave incorrect odds!

Always remember that just because something is in a book, that doesn't mean it's correct.

All the information in *this* book, in regard to things that I personally was connected with, is the Real McCoy. I give you my personal guarantee on that. On stories that I picked up from the media I usually identify my sources, and I've saved all the clippings whenever I could, so I can back up my reports as far as they go. Want proof? You can write me in care of the publisher and I'll send you documentation where available.

Not every author is so careful in checking sources. Years ago I sat down with a friend of mine who was writing a book on literary censorship, and I let him pick my brain. I pride myself on being very knowledgeable on the subject. Knowledgeable yes, but, as it turned out, not infallible. Somewhere along the way I had learned of the existence of a pornographic operetta by Gilbert & Sullivan, commissioned by Queen Victoria entitled *The Sod's Opera*. The original manuscript was reported to be safeguarded in a locked bookcase in the British Museum's Private Cabinet. This x-rated piece was said to have typically clever Gilbert & Sullivan characters such as Scrotum, An Old Retainer; The Bollox Brothers, "A Pair of Hangers-on at the Court. . . ." You get the picture. Without checking, my friend put it all into his book.

Twenty-five years later, I have seen it reprinted in more than a dozen books, here and abroad. The only problem is that the x-rated operetta by Gilbert & Sullivan doesn't exist! A couple of years after the book was published I met the world's foremost authority on Gilbert & Sullivan, who informed me that the story was pure hoax.

This is why you have to be wary of information that you read in a book, especially in a gambling book.

Introduction
I'm Not a Gambler

I never expected to write a book on gambling. Me, I'm just a guy who's been gambling in casinos since the spring of 1960, when my friend Lyle Stuart talked me into flying to Las Vegas from New York—a daring endeavor and extraordinary then in those days of mostly propeller-driven planes. This, for a scant three days and two nights, all just to see a legendary casino show that would become known as "The Summit Meeting." It starred Frank Sinatra, Dean Martin, Sammy Davis, Jr., Peter Lawford, and Joey Bishop. By night they performed together on stage at the Sands, while by day they were filming *Ocean's 11*. Forty years and hundreds of casinos later, I have to admit that I haven't seen a better casino show since that first one. Gambling-wise, I've done a lot better since, but it was a torturous—and rather expensive—journey. In retrospect, what it cost me in blood money—money that at one point I couldn't afford to lose—amounted to the dues I paid to reach where I am today.

What I am going to tell you in this book will save you a lot of dollars. I'll confess the costly mistakes I've made so that you can avoid them. The information I offer cost me many thousands of dollars in pitfalls and pratfalls along the way. I finally wised up, but it was an expensive journey. I learned it the hard way, but I can help you to learn it the easy way.

A gambler who lies to himself and to others is doomed forever to dwell among the ranks of losers. If you gamble and you want to enter the thinly populated world of the winners, learn that you cannot live in the bullshit dimension. Don't imitate the casinos. They tell you "their" casino is "The friendliest" in Atlantic City or Las Vegas, that "they" want you to come (with your bankroll) and "feel like part of the family."

It's all sham.

The casinos play hardball all the time. If you want to have a chance to beat them at their own games, you must understand that they are suckering you. Keep your wits about you at all times, until you're safely heading home with your winnings. With my two no-hitters against the casinos in a little over two months, I can write with a modicum of authority.

Don't get me wrong. Arrogance and smug self-assurance are the quicksand that'll gobble up a gambler's bankroll. I never approach a gambling table without the utmost caution—the same caution with which I would approach a bear trap. On May 16, 1999, I played at fourteen blackjack tables in twelve casinos in a row in one day without a loss. At the fourteenth table—my last table for the day—I exercised as much caution in playing as I did at my first table, when I was fresh off the bus from New York.

This book is not only about blackjack. I will share with you my experiences with every game in the casino, including my one-time love/hate relationships with Keno and the money-hungry slot machines. I'll even tell you about one flawed slot machine that I emptied out, and how I had the sweet thrill of watching the sour-faced attendant turn the depleted machine to the wall.

Some of what I write is anecdotal. I will relate my adventures in dozens of casinos, from Monte Carlo and Nice, to Reno and Waldorf, Maryland, as well as my stints in illegal casinos in Hot Springs, Arkansas. I'll tell you about times I was cheated—yes, cheated—in Atlantic City and in Las Vegas—and the times dishonest casino employees cheated the casinos in my favor, hoping for a handsome "toke" (tip).

I'll also tell you about the honesty of one casino—how my Keno ticket was worth a thousand dollars more than I thought, and how they went out of their way to upgrade my ticket and pay me every dollar due me.

In addition to all this, I want to assure you that I'm not a compulsive gambler.

I've never been to a race track. I agree with legendary gambler Nick the Greek: Never bet on anything that eats.

I don't buy lottery tickets—though I've collected lottery money prizes five times in my life, including a $1300 Lotto ticket! But more about that later.

I don't play poker with the boys.

I shy away from office baseball and football pools.

I've only bet once at OTB (Off-Track Betting) in New York, and I quit winners.

I didn't even pitch pennies with the kids in grade school.

But yes, I do gamble at the casinos, and I've been doing it for four decades. When I first went to the Las Vegas Sands in 1960, I was wide-eyed and hell-bent to break the bank. The one who ended up broke was me, and I was lucky to have enough left for cab fare back from the airport to my apartment. Parenthetically, in New York, before the days of the lotteries, the East Coast casinos and OTB, the race tracks were the serious gambler's only refuge. There are stories about horseplayers that lost their shirts at the track who had the foresight to put a nickel—subways were a nickel then—in a rented ten-cent locker to insure having the fare for the return trip home.

Today I go to the casinos with an entirely different mind-set. No, I don't want to clean out their cashier cages, or take home their chandeliers, I only want to nibble away at them. Hit and run—Lyle Stuart taught it to me—and that's the only way I know to beat the casinos. Years ago, during a weekend at Caesars Palace, I was strolling over to the elevator when I saw a heavy-set man sitting—yes, sitting—at the end of a craps table. In front of him, piled on the racks and on the table itself, was the highest mountain of chips I have ever seen in front of one player. He appeared to be playing almost everything on the table—all the numbers, proposition bets, the field—the works. I watched for a few minutes and then went to my room for some shut-eye. Six hours later I returned to the casino. The fellow was still there, sitting in front of his chips . . . only now there was no mountain—it was barely a molehill—a lot fewer chips there than there were the night before. Here was a man who should have hit and run hours ago.

In his book on gambling, John Scarne tells the lesson-to-be-learned classic story of the busboy from a Strip casino who took his paycheck downtown to the Fremont Street casinos. Lady Luck smiled on him as he gambled through the night and miraculously worked his meager bankroll up to $50,000. Toward dawn his luck turned sour and—you guessed it—he lost it all, sadly drag-assing himself at 9:00 A.M. back to his menial busboy job on the Strip. Scarne then astutely noted that, even if the busboy had run up his bankroll to $75,000 or even $100,000 or more, he would have doggedly stayed at the tables until he was completely tapped out. I read it years ago, and never forgot the lesson I learned there. I hope you'll always remember it too.

Hit and Run

How to Hit and Run

Thumb through any of the gambling magazines that have prolif- erated in recent years and you'll see page after page of ads from self-proclaimed experts who, for a fee of anything from ten bucks to a thousand, will sell you the in-secrets of beating the table games, or beating the slots.

Now take a deep breath and reread the above paragraph. Do you really believe in your heart-of-hearts that, if these advertis- ers *really* knew any sure-fire ways to consistently win money from the casinos, they would let you in on their secrets? Believe me, pal, if any alleged know-it-all hotshot actually stumbled upon a way to beat the casinos at their own games, you could hang him by his thumbs and shove a hot poker up his ass and he *still* wouldn't tell you!

After forty years of casino gambling the only way I know to beat 'em is to hit and run, always wary of "staying too long at the fair."

Make sure your goal is to Quit Winners and, dammit, to stick to your predetermined win figure. Yes, I know: You're on a "streak" and you're raking in the chips. Sure, it's hard as hell to tear yourself away from the table. But you have set a limit on what you want to win, and now you have to be man or woman enough to stick to it. Having reached your predetermined goal, simply pick up your chips, cash them in, and head directly out the door, off to the next casino. If you overstay your welcome, you are in dire peril not only of losing what you won, but also your table stakes as well.

Once at the Stardust in Las Vegas, before the prevalence of purple or white ($500) and orange or yellow ($1,000) chips, black chips ($100) were generally the top unit of wagering at the tables. Gamblers strolled the casino with the wooden racks now used for dollar slot machine tokens. I was doing very nicely, thank you, with my tray almost completely filled with blacks. Two more steps away from the cashier's cage, I decided, what the hell, I needed to win just two more blacks to fill it up and make it a neat $5,000.

Twenty minutes later I put the empty wooden tray on top of a slot machine and sadly shuffled out the door. Had I stuck to my guns and not tried to get those extra two chips, I would have quit winners. Learn from me: If you've got your projected squeeze from the udder of the casino cash-cow, leave with their money. Don't overstay your welcome, else you'll be dumping your empty wooden tray on top of a slot machine as you drag-ass out of the casino door, a loser just like me.

When I go to the casinos, I play a nibble-away game. As I write, there are twelve licensed casinos in Atlantic City, but actually thirteen operating casinos. One of the licensees, Bally's, finessed the Casino Control Commission by appending a satellite casino to an operating casino, thus having two casinos working on one license. (Trump tried it, and tacked the old Playboy, then the Atlantis, onto his Plaza, but went bust.) Bally's Park Place erected a brand-new casino, the Wild West, and built a connecting passageway between the two.

For me, the more casinos on the block, the merrier. Once I went to Connecticut and tried my luck at the Native American

Foxwoods Casino. Never again, thank you. If Foxwoods was the only casino around, I'd hang up my hiking boots and quit gambling. But don't get me wrong: I have nothing against Foxwoods or Native Americans. It's just that if I'm limited to gambling in only one casino, I am fated to join the swelling ranks of losers. When Foxwoods was the only casino in all of the northeastern section of the country, it was the most profitable casino in America—and I don't find that coincidental. When the word got around about the roaring success of Foxwoods, a rival tribe down the road in Connecticut decided they also wanted to get in on a good thing. So now there are two Indian casinos in that neck of the woods. Not to be left out, a New York State Indian tribe has also set up shop near Syracuse. So competition may bring better odds to Foxwoods.

My only chance of winning is to keep putting mileage on my hiking shoes. I have to be able to pick up my chips and hightail it over to the next casino at a moment's notice.

All my hit-and-run trips to Vegas and Atlantic City were carefully time-controlled. I always had one eye on the dice or the blackjack hand and the other eye on my wristwatch. I always made absolutely sure I allowed myself enough time to make that plane or bus. I never ever, on my Lone Wolf prowls, missed my return mode of transportation, but I must admit there were squeakers. One time in particular was just too close for comfort. It was the end of a one-day raid on the Las Vegas casinos for a specific goal— I needed some quick cash for the next day. I had taken my ever-faithful TWA Flight #57 at 5:30 from Kennedy to McCarran, with a return flight on the last plane out to New York that midnight. I had done well so far on my hit-and-run journey up the Strip from the Sahara, and now I was at the Aladdin, my final casino before cabbing to the airport. (This was in the 1970's, when both blackjack and craps limits were in the hundreds, and purple ($500) chips were only seen on the baccarat table.) Nicely ahead for the evening,

I cashed a couple of thousand in seed money at the blackjack table as the dice came around to me. Playing the front line with, of course, full odds—along with placing the 6 and 8, I took control of the dice. This was going to be my Grand Finale for the evening, a quick win at the table and a quicker exit out the door and off to the airport.

My point was 10. I wound up like Sandy Koufax, and sent the cubes hurtling down the table, bouncing smartly against the back wall.

The number was 3. Again I rolled them cubes, and again it was a no-decision (for me) 12.

And I rolled again. And again. And still again.

Still no decision. I was nowhere near my needed 10.

Time was ticking away, and I was getting nervous. I started to roll faster. In fact, for the first time in my casino career I asked the stickman to please speed up the action. Now it was getting hairy. I took down my two place bets, and even picked up my odds bet just to show the stickman my urgency and sincerity in trying to finish the roll as soon as possible. Three more rolls and still no decision.

In desperation I pleaded, "Look, I gotta make a plane. Any way that I can just cede the hand and split?"

The table went into an uproar. My notion that I could escape was an impossible dream. To make matters worse, the other players at the table became menacing.

"Roll them cubes, shithead."

"Finish off the hand and buzz off. We don't want you around here either."

I rolled and rolled and finally sevened out. Believe me, I was never so happy to lose. Not to waste a minute, I shoveled the chips into my pockets and raced for the exit. Who had time to cash them in? I barely made the plane—I was the last one to board—and had a double vodka when the hostess came around with the beverage cart. Believe me, I needed it.

There was yet another time I just made the plane by a hair, but there wasn't a pocket full of black chips involved—just a ball-busting suitcase full of nickels. Yes, nickels, and lots of 'em.

Let me explain. One of my pit stops on the way to the airport was the Dunes. At the time they had a gimmicky slot machine promotion to bring in the locals—a pregnant nickel machine with a twin (or was it triple?) jackpot. The machine was bulging with nickels, with nickels showing everywhere. Man, did it look tempting! Every time I passed the damn machine I put my five nickels in, hoping to hit the jackpot. Always without luck. That is, until my little pit stop on the way to the airport.

You guessed it—I hit the Super-Duper Nickel Jackpot! I didn't believe that there were that many fucking nickels in the whole world. I looked over and saw that the line for the Coin Cashier wound around the corner. Happily, my carry-on luggage was strong, so in the middle of the Dunes casino I opened it up and started tossing out expendables—two Las Vegas newspapers, my subscription copies of *Playboy* and *Penthouse*, my big can of shaving cream, plus other trifles that could be replaced in Manhattan. Then I started pouring in the nickels. Pouring is the correct word, as I used one of the heavy cardboard cups placed between the slots by every casino, to scoop and pour the nickels into my suitcase. They all fit, but the goddam thing weighed a ton. It was like carrying an anvil.

Somehow I managed to get it onto the plane and somehow I finally got it home. Then I poured my winnings out in the middle of my living room floor. God, for a mass of nickels it really looked impressive! Needless to say, it was a long, long time before I ever had to ask anybody to change a quarter.

The moral of all this is: Always remember to wear a watch and keep a keen eye on it. Casinos have no windows and no clocks, all carefully planned to keep the player in a time-warp limbo. To quit winners, you always have to stay one step ahead of the casino.

And, always bear in mind that the casinos are open seven-days-a-week, twenty-four-hours-a-day, all at *your* convenience. They only have an opportunity to get a crack at your bankroll when *you* choose to put it on the line. You must always remember that! Never lose sight of it. It's *your* choice *when* and *where* you play, and for *how long*, and for *how much*.

♠ ♠ ♠ ♠ ♠

My most hectic hit-and-run foray into Vegas was in the early 1960s, when I arrived in the midst of a taxi strike. I have a driver's license, but damned if I would take a chance renting a car for a few hours in Las Vegas, even if a rental car was available. Large Army-style buses awaited arrivals, taking visitors on a casino-to-casino route, a round-robin of a trip, and then back to the airport. What could I do? What I did do was, every time the bus made a stop, I'd race into the casino, make a quick bet or two at the first open blackjack table nearest the door, and race right back to the bus. Sure, I had a couple of close calls, nearly missing the bus, but I insured my bet with the driver by tokening him with a green chip from the first casino and promising him another one when we reached the last casino on his route. I made about a thousand dollars over expenses, but I lost five pounds with all the to-do, and I have to record it as the hardest buck I ever made in Las Vegas.

♠ ♠ ♠ ♠ ♠

Before we talk about what and what not to do when you gamble in casinos, let's first pay tribute to my personal Patron Saint of the Green-Felt Tables, Louis G. Holloway. Mr. Holloway lived and raised a family in Las Vegas, where he gambled for his livelihood. He also wrote a splendid book entitled *Full-Time Gambler*. Holloway was a low-key, low-profile player, who made the rounds of the

Vegas casinos for an hour or two daily, winning a few dollars here, winning a few dollars there.

When his MIT-graduate son insisted that no one can beat the casinos, Holloway replied, "Son, do you see this house? The car outside? The nice clothes we're wearing? Gambling paid for all of it, including paying for your college tuition."

The Rules of Hit and Run

My first rule in casino gambling is: Never bet with "scared money." Scared money rarely wins. Your investment capital (that's what you must consider it) should consist of "mad money"—money that, if you lose it, won't affect your lifestyle. If the cards and dice don't go your way, tough! When I lose and, yes, there are times I do lose—I just shrug my shoulders and tell myself "tomorrow is another day. . . ." Victor Lownes, who ran the Playboy Casino in London when it was the most profitable casino in the world, aptly phrased it when he advised that, if you lose, just consider it "expensive entertainment."

My second basic rule is: Never take credit. Casino hosts masquerading as your friendly Dutch Uncles are eager to set up a credit line for you. Beware! Don't—I repeat, do not—ever bite the bait. If you do, you will live to regret it. Through the years enough credit has been offered me to buy the Empire State Building. In forty years of casino gambling, I have yet to swallow the hook, not even once.

Take special note of my next rule: Your credit cards enable you to ravage the ATM machines that are conveniently located throughout casinos: LEAVE ALL YOUR CREDIT CARDS AT HOME! If you must carry a card with you, take one that *doesn't* give access to ATM machines. Sure, there have been times when the dice went against me and my working capital was wiped out. But I never used my plastic card to restock the plastic chips, though I sometimes had to use it to buy a meal, or even a wee drop of the grape. (Yes, occasionally I do take a drink or two to help restart my motor. After three or four hours of casino-hopping a vodka-and-tonic tastes great. Still, if alcohol affects you adversely, stay away.)

As for the ever-conspicuous ATM machines in the casinos, I sometimes stand and watch those sad souls standing in line awaiting their turn to take money out of *one* casino machine, just to put it into *another* casino machine. And most probably never to see it again.

If you're going to Atlantic City or Las Vegas for a weekend, split your bankroll into three equal packs—one for each day of your stay. Put one pack in your pocket and the other two in the hotel safe. Don't imitate the hotshot from California who went to Vegas for a weekend. While his wife was waiting on line to check in, he hightailed it over to the craps table. Before she even got to the registration desk he meekly sidled over to her and said, "We're going home, honey. I just blew our bankroll."

My Biggest Win

" . . . [W]hen one is lucky and running lucky, one can do no wrong and suffer no loss! . . . We keep telling him that the law of probabilities will eventually grind him out. And he laughs at us as he counts his winnings."

This from the July 1, 1969, issue of *The High Roller*, the much-respected, now regrettably defunct gambling newsletter of the 1960s. Looking back at what was written about me thirty years ago, I can only concur with the editor, on both counts.

Checking over the score card now, I shudder at my foolhardy onslaught on the Las Vegas casinos. As they say in the crude vernacular, I must have stepped in shit to have run rampant through the casinos in a nonstop, three-day rampage. Amazingly, I got back on the plane safely with $31,125 of their money.

Not only did I consistently win in casino after casino, but I ducked in and out of the *same* casino multiple times; *four* times in the case of the Sahara!

And I did it all on craps, a game I rarely play these days.

Looking back at it all now, in the cold light of July, 2000, I can attribute it either to youthful naïveté or temporary madness.

Examine my scorecard, along with the story about me and my win in *The High Roller*, which I reprint in its entirety. As the editor wanted to protect my privacy he dubbed me "Lucky Pierre." The facts are true; only the name was changed to protect the player. (With the wild roller coaster ride I foolishly went on in my helter-skelter three-day casino spree, the editor should have dubbed me "Reckless Pierre.")

I include this curious and aberrant episode as a warning to the reader to avoid such wild and reckless forays. Sure, I challenged the dragon and slew him, but if you foolishly follow in my footsteps, I guarantee the dragon will chew on your ass for dinner.

Postscript: In a subsequent issue, *The High Roller* scolded me for returning to casinos where I'd been unlucky and losing.

"[He] finds a casino where [he] does good, and wins their money. [Then he] finds a casino where [he's] consistently unlucky, where [he] can't even win a slab of gum from the penny gum machine. Instead of taking the lucky casino for everything [he] can, [he] wins big there, and then goes to the unlucky place and drops it."

Thank you, Mr. Editor. I subsequently took your sage advice and profited from the information.

I hope you will profit from this savvy gambling tip, too.

From *THE HIGH ROLLER*, July 1, 1969

Our Hero Does It Again

In past issues we have described the true-to-life tale of a joyful gambler who paid short visits to Vegas and more often than not, came away with winnings. *The High Roller* was peculiarly impressed because the facts were absolutely true and verified by us.

We keep telling him that he can't win . . . that the law of probabilities will eventually grind him out. And he laughs at us as he counts his winnings.

Last week he paid another visit to Las Vegas. Here is a play-by-play score card, with only a few changes to protect his identity. We'll call our hero Lucky Pierre—for what follows certainly illustrates the fact that when one is lucky and running lucky, one can do no wrong and suffer no loss! The way our hero plays has been described in a previous issue of *The High Roller*. We won't repeat that . . . except to remind you that he plays nothing but dice.

On the first day in town, Lucky Pierre decided to visit a number of casinos and see if he could "hit them all for $200 each." His starting bankroll was just under $4,000.

For the first hour, he had four bouts with the Sahara and ended up $1,300 ahead. The Thunderbird was good for $650. The Riviera allowed him to pocket $2,350. The Desert Inn was good for $3,500 on this visit. $2,600 was the amount he picked up at The Stardust.

He suffered the first loss at The Riviera and attributes this to his own greed. Having won $300—or $100 more than his goal, he turned around and went back to the tables to drop $2,700.

Downtown to Fremont Street and the Horseshoe. $1,300. By cab to The Sands for an even $1,000. To the end of the gaming strip and the Tropicana for $800. It was now early A.M. and our exhausted hero decided to call it a night. He had ended ahead $11,100.

On the second day, he hit the Sahara again for $1,900. With this nice beginning he took a stroll to the Thunderbird to pick up $1,700. Now he ran into his first reversal of the day. Ahead $14,700 when he entered its portals, he dropped $5,700 at the Dunes. He returned minutes later to give them another $800. On the street he became angry with himself and returned again. Did our hero, now caught up in his emotions, drop it all? No, Lucky Pierre won $4,000.

The Sahara was good for $3,600. Caesars Palace for $500. At this point, our hero was $16,300 ahead of the game. So what did he do? Of course! He returned to challenge the Dunes again.

Less than an hour later, he was $12,100 the poorer, though still a winner overall to the amount of $4,200. In a taxi to the Desert Inn. At the door he hailed another cab and returned to the Dunes. He dropped another $900. Now he was $2,300 ahead. He took a walk and considered catching the next plane home. When he looked up, he was back at the Dunes. Anyone else would have lost the winnings and the bankroll, too, at this point—or be wise enough to run the other way. Our hero went inside and won $3,300.

With a happy smile, he headed for the Sands where he picked up another $4,800. And then to the Sahara for a nightcap and $1,900. He actually ended his second day with $12,500 in winnings—or $1,400 ahead of the day before.

On the third and last day, nothing went wrong. His "goal" had long before been raised from $200 per casino to $1,000 per casino. In rapid succession he visited the Sahara for $5,700; the Desert Inn to win $5,300. The Sahara gave him $1,300. The Flamingo another $4,300. The Dunes another $5,900. Checking out of the Sahara, he picked up another $1125. At the Airport, he dropped a nickel in the slot machine. A loser. And so he left Las Vegas $31,125 ahead—unless you want to deduct that nickel!

"Lucky Pierre's" most winning score card (June, 1969)

DAY #1

CASINO	SHOOT FOR	ACTUAL	RUNNING TOTAL
Sahara	200	+400	+400
Sahara	200	+300	+700
Sahara	200	+450	+1,150
Sahara	200	+150	+1,300
Thunderbird	200	+650	+1,950
Riviera	200	+2,350	+4,300
Desert Inn	200	+3,500	+7,800
Stardust	200	+1,000	+8,800
Stardust	200	+1,200	+10,000
Stardust	200	+400	+10,400
Riviera	200	+300	+10,700
Riviera	200	-2,700	+8,000
Horseshoe	200	+1,300	+9,300
Sands	200	+1,000	+10,300
Tropicana	200	+800	+11,100

DAY #2

CASINO	SHOOT FOR	ACTUAL	RUNNING TOTAL
Sahara	200	+1,900	+13,000
Thunderbird	200	+1,700	+14,700
Dunes	200	-5,700	+9,000
Dunes	1,000	-800	+8,200
Dunes	1,000	+4,000	+12,200
Sahara	1,000	+3,600	+15,800
Caesars	1,000	+500	+16,300
Dunes	100	-12,100	+4,200
Dunes	1,000	-900	+2,300
Dunes	100	+3,300	+5,800
Sands	1,000	+4,800	+10,600
Sahara	1,000	+1,900	+12,500

DAY #3

Sahara	1,000	+3,200	+15,700
Sahara	1,000	+2,500	+18,200
Desert Inn	1,000	+2,500	+20,700
Desert Inn	1,000	+600	+21,300
Desert Inn	1,000	-2,200	+19,100
Sahara	1,000	+1,300	+20,400
Flamingo	1,000	+4,300	+24,100
Dunes	500	+500	+24,600
Dunes	1,000	+5,400	+30,000
Sahara	1,000	+1,125	+31,125

My three day Las Vegas Spree where it seemed I could do no wrong!

Shoot For: What my goal was in the casino.
Actual: What the monetary outcome actually was.

You Ain't Dead 'Til Your Ass Is Cold

When I first got a seat on the casino roller coaster in 1950, I was still wet behind my ears. Sure, I read John Scarne's big book on casino gambling and listened attentively at Lyle Stuart's knee. However, my on-the-job training came in the casinos themselves. As much as Scarne and Stuart taught me, wagering at real tables and playing real slot machines gave me an entirely new dimension of understanding.

I never took much money along—I didn't have that much disposable cash to begin with—so my early forays, though mostly losers, weren't financially crushing. On my very first trip in 1960 I mainly stuck to the slot machines; blackjack was an exotic, slightly intimidating experience that I approached cautiously—and only at the $2 tables. I didn't dare venture over to the $5 tables.

When I started to get a handle on the casino swing of things, I became emboldened to do foolhardy things that I wouldn't dare do today. I won money fast and I lost money fast. With these wild fluctuations in my bankroll, the only thing that kept me out of bankruptcy court was my iron-clad resolution to never—but never—play with scared money and never—but never—take credit. My last resolution was sometimes sorely tested when I was in Vegas with Lyle. Tagging along with the legendary High Roller, I was offered financial courtesies that I never would have been offered if I was by myself. Being with Stuart I was offered instant, on-the-spot credit, just on Lyle's say-so. Prudently, I always passed on these golden opportunities, though having a sudden influx of easy, heavy seed money right at the tables was always tantalizingly tempting.

While my point here is to discourage betting with borrowed money, I can't resist relating one exception. A friend of mine once told me about his uncle who worked as a teller in a bank in the days before computers and the proliferation of casinos. A horse-racing addict who fancied himself an ace handicapper, the teller would dip into the till on Fridays when the nags were running, and first thing Monday mornings would quietly return the "borrowed" money. My friend said his uncle retired a wealthy man, never having once been detected in his bank-financed racetrack escapades.

My stubborn refusal of credit was always my saving grace. When I lost, I lost what I could afford, period. Once my seed money was swept away on wagers I didn't win, that was it. I was tapped out, tapioca, as Manhattan saloonkeeper Toots Shor put it. If I had time to kill till the next bus left, I only played the slot machines—usually the nickel ones—till departure time.

Once, just once, at Atlantic City's Park Place, I was just about tapped out and so I invested my last $10 in seed money in a roll of quarters. I idly played a 25-cent slot machine, nursing the pile of quarters for quite a while, with a spate of small wins. Suddenly, like the phoenix, I arose from the ashes and hit a $750 jackpot!

Emboldened by the windfall of quarters, I decided to upgrade my play and resolutely headed directly to the dollar machines. A couple of $500 hits and a spectacular $1,000 jackpot later, I was suddenly a player with a bankroll, ready for action again at the blackjack tables.

I wish I could give this casino Cinderella story a happy ending, but it turned out that my late financial resurgence that day was all for naught. I ended up sadly replaying my earlier misfortunes at the tables, back where I started from, only now $10 poorer with my last roll of quarters gone too. I sadly shuffled over to the bus terminal with my return ticket and just enough pocket money to see me safely back to my Manhattan apartment. Though this foray was a two-act loser, it does show that you're not dead 'til your ass is cold.

On the flip side, you should never count your chickens before they hatch, especially in a casino. Once in the late 1960s, my early freewheeling days, I gambled through two tumultuous days and nights, storming in and out of Las Vegas casinos, and I ended up with $24,000 of the casinos' money. Up in my Sahara suite, $100 bills piled high on the table, I soberly reviewed the situation. I realized I was too hopped up for my own good, so, after a much-needed night's sleep, I dumped most of the money in a casino safe-deposit box and wisely decided to plane out to San Francisco for the day. I always wanted to sample their King Crab claws on Fisherman's Wharf. I really dig those King Crab claws!

Refreshed and well crab-clawed, I took an early-evening flight back to Las Vegas and the green-felt tables. Dame Fortune can be fickle, and with me she was then at her worst. Almost as soon as I started betting once again—and this was at my darling, always-profitable Sahara—I found myself on a tail-spinning losing streak that I just couldn't buck. To "change my luck," as the saying goes, I even took a $22 cab ride up from the bottom of the Strip all the way over to the other end of the world—The Hacienda, the first casino at the top of the Strip.

You think that did it? Sadly it did not, as my losing streak continued, relentlessly on-course, whatever casino I went to, whatever I bet, whether at blackjack or at craps. I couldn't even coax more than a couple of coins at a time out of the damn slot machines!

The only reason I returned to New York with my seed money still intact and with $3,300 of the casinos' cash, was that I had bragged to one of my girl friends that I would win enough money on this trip to be able to fly her out the following week to Vegas to see Sinatra at the Sands. I sure as hell would've felt like a horse's ass to have to tell her we're going by subway to Coney Island instead, only to fill up on hot dogs and beer. Just my ego kept me from losing that last $3,300.

Sure, looking back on my trip in retrospect, I can bemoan the fact that my post-San Francisco casino-hopping cost me more than $20,000. But I don't. I quote Harold of Harolds Club in Reno, and only see the trip positively. "I quit winners!"

What you can learn from all this is to make sure that you leave the casinos with at least *some* of their money. This way, when you're on the bus or plane, you can say, "Yes, I quit winners!"

"Won't" Power

Shouldn't Will Power really be called "Won't" Power, as in "I WON'T do it"? Once, just to test myself, I bused to Atlantic City with the firm determination to ONLY win $1,500. Not $1,550. Only $1,500. Period. Needless to say, I played it especially carefully, and kept an extra careful score card. My sixth casino that afternoon was Resorts, home of the famous clam bar that featured the best King Crab claws in town—my one seafood weakness.

I was only $235 away from my $1,500 goal. A $235 bet on a "hard" 17—the dealer showed a five—was a winner when the dealer busted. Now I had a dilemma: Should I break my promise to myself and place another bet of two green chips—$50—to "comp" myself for the crab claw feast awaiting me just a few steps from the casino entrance?

I suddenly remembered that black day at the Stardust in Las Vegas fifteen years earlier. That was when, heading for the cashier's cage, I saw that all I "only" needed were two more black chips to neatly fill my $5,000 tray. That's when I left my now-empty tray on top of a slot machine. Wary of a repeat performance, I prudently decided this time to dig into my wallet and splurged as I treated myself to a hearty order of King Crab claws, along with a tall frosty stein of draft beer.

♠ ♠ ♠ ♠ ♠

There is a very valid, logical reason for both Vegas and Atlantic City to have windowless and clockless casinos. With no clocks and no windows, Time in the casino has no dimension for the player. Day or night, it's always the same time in the casino. That's why earlier in this book I emphasize the importance of having a wristwatch with you on your casino visits.

In all my casino years, most all payout booths generally have been located as far back as possible in the casino. When you pause and think about it, you have to admit it is a clever ploy on the casino's part. When you cash out, and turn around headed to the exit, you have to pass a gauntlet of gambling games, plus rows of enticing slot machines. Oh, how many times in the early days did I win it, and then lose it all back on my way out of the casino! Even now, occasionally I'll daringly hit-and-run at a blackjack table I'm passing on the way out just to "even up" a total, i.e., turn $385 into $400, or to try to win a green ($25) chip to dabble at the slots before I venture to the next casino. My advice here is to do as I *say*, not as I *do*. If you won your predetermined amount, cash out and GO! Wear blinkers if you have to, but haul your ass out the door, and off to the next casino.

Yesterday at my local fish store I bought a pound of Alaskan crab claws. Like a cat loves cream, I go ga-ga for crab claws. I suspect that, to exploit this weakness, a clever casino-baited trap was set for me, and I was always eager to fall into it. In Las Vegas decades ago I used to win pretty regularly at "my" Sahara. It was my cash-cow. I'd then go off to the Thunderbird, now just a Vegas memory. The T-Bird wasn't one of my A-list casinos, but I'd often head straight to their small and cozy seafood bar for their mouth-watering King Crab claws.

When I bussed into Atlantic City, there was only one casino I always made sure to stop at: Resorts International. You guessed it, they had a cozy little seafood bar where I gorged myself on their succulent King Crab claws. Any gambling money I have spent there was really snapped up by the crabs!

Going to a casino for a meal can be an adventure. At Resorts I always went the same route: Right off the bat I'd win a couple of green chips, just enough for me to pig out with a plate load of King Crab claws, a bowl of clam chowder, and a small bottle of red wine. (Yes, I know it is *de rigueur* to have white wine with fish, but I happen to like red wine with my crab claws, thank you.) Most of the time I easily made my modest meal-money goal, and then headed straight to the seafood bar with my two green chips. But occasionally, just occasionally, disaster did strike, and it ended up costing me a king's ransom for my plate of King Crabs.

For me, the seafood bar was a fur-lined bear trap. For you, the bait may take a different shape. There are a hundred other casino enticements, promotions, freebies, and star entertainers, to name a few—all designed to get you inside. Loss-leader buffets, gratis gifts, a complimentary pull on a Million Dollar Slot, even free money, just to lure you in. Some casinos will go so far as to refund your cash on adverse slot machine action. I once got suckered into such a promotion . . . but that's a chapter in itself.

Watch Walt Disney's cartoon feature *Pinocchio*, where the little wooden boy gets lured onto Pleasure Island, only to end up being turned into a braying ass. Make sure you don't get brainwashed by casino enticements into doing stupid things too. Don't empty your wallet and turn yourself into a horse's ass.

The Cautionary Tale of Joe E. Lewis

Joe E. Lewis, great saloon entertainer and notorious compulsive gambler, was dining with a chorus girl at the Sands. Running out of cigarettes, the chorine asked Lewis if he'd mind getting her a fresh pack at the smoke shop just off the casino. He got up and left, returning in a few minutes with the smokes. As they were getting up to leave, Lewis picked up the open pack and handed it to her "Better take 'em with you, honey. They cost me $32,000."

Blackjack

✓ The Game of 21
✓ Practical Examples
✓ Seed Money
✓ A Tip
✓ Dumb Luck

The Game of 21

I should assume that the reader has a working knowledge of blackjack, but being a casino habitué for forty years I have learned to assume nothing.

Blackjack is a simple game built on a simple concept. The player's object is to get a higher total than the Dealer, but not to exceed the sum of 21.

Today, partly to frustrate card counters, most casinos use a "shoe" that contains six or eight decks of cards. The shoe is an elongated plastic or wooden box with a clear plastic cover. It allows the dealer to deal from it, one card at a time. Once the decks of cards are shuffled and "cut" by the player, the cards are placed in the shoe, and the game is ready to begin. It must be said that cutting the cards is not a gilt-edged guarantee that the cards aren't stacked. The hand is quicker than the eye, and a good "mechanic" can easily "fix" a deck right in front of you.

Later I'll tell you about an episode that turned me off forever from playing blackjack in any hand-held dealing games.

To begin a game of blackjack, the player places his bet on the designated space on the cloth in front of him. The dealer then deals a card face-up to the player and a card face-up to himself.

The dealer now deals a second face-up card to the player, but for himself he deals the card face-down and tucks it under his open card. This is the dealer's hidden "hole" card. The numerical value of the cards dealt corresponds with what is printed on them, with the exception of the picture cards (Jacks, Queens, and Kings), which are all counted as ten-pointers, and the Ace, which has a value of one or eleven, player's choice.

Now the cards are out. If the player gets an Ace along with a ten or picture card, he has a "blackjack," and promptly receives one-and-a-half times his wager. If, however, the dealer also gets a blackjack, it is a "Mexican Standoff"—a tie game that neither dealer nor player wins or loses. In fact, if the player and dealer have any identical amount, it's a "push" and nobody wins.

If neither the dealer nor the player gets a blackjack, the game proceeds. Depending on his two-card total, the player may request a "hit," meaning an additional card, or several "hits," depending on his judgment of his two-card count and the dealer's "open" card. This is an advantage for the player, as he has the discretion of hitting or standing pat (staying) with his hand, while the dealer is boxed-in with iron-clad rules that compel him to hit *any* total up to and including 16, and requiring him to stand on any total of 17 or more. In other words, if the player has 18 and the dealer has a total of 17, the dealer cannot draw another card to try to beat him. The dealer's advantage, however, is that if the player draws and "busts" (gets a total of more than 21) the dealer takes his money even if, after dealing to other players, he draws and busts too.

The bare rule-of-thumb basic strategy in the game is for the player to hit if his total is 16 or less when the dealer shows a 7, 8, 9, or 10 value card, or an Ace. With eight decks there are *lots* of 10 value cards in the shoe, so the player has to assume a 10 or a picture card as the dealer's hole card. On the other hand, if the dealer shows a 4, 5, or a 6, basic strategy is for the player to "stand," and to let the dealer draw and possibly bust.

When the dealer shows a 2 or a 3, you face a choice. Here's where I differ from many so-called blackjack experts. When single or double decks were more common years ago, I'd stand on the dealer's 2 or 3. Now, with the 8-deck shoe, I *have* to swim against the current of the prevailing wisdom mentioned above—to consider the dealer's hole card a 10 spot. With all the cards that can help the dealer's total on a 2 showing, I *always* hit my 12 or 13 count.

As for insurance, surrender, and "Let It Ride," forget it. All three are bad, bad bets. If you want more details about these three sucker bets you are welcome to read all about them in another blackjack book. I won't waste time on these shams.

While the dealer is rigidly constricted by his options, the player is allowed splendid leeway which, if managed properly, can be a decided advantage to him in the game.

First, there is the player's option of splitting pairs. When the player is dealt two identical cards, he may separate them, making them the first cards of two separate hands. Sometimes it's an advantage and sometimes it isn't. The only hard-and-set rule for splitting pairs is with Aces and 8's, which the player should almost always split. Exception: Where the dealer shows an Ace, an 8, 9, or a 10 point card, I don't split 8's. If the dealer shows a 5 or a 6, it is advantageous for the player to split *all* pairs—I even split 10 point pairs in this case, which can be construed as either daring or lunatic. (Many times I shake up the pit boss when I split 10 pointers; it's done so infrequently that they are often rattled by my move.) In some casinos you can split a third time (except with aces), and if the same card shows up a *fourth* time, some casinos will even let you split it still again. In the next section I will give you graphic examples of what can and does happen with multiple splittings.

Practical Examples

Now that I've given you all the standard rules, and some variations of mine that have served me well, let's show it all in action, with chips in play.

You're at a blackjack table, the only player. It is a "No Mid-Entry" table—nobody can enter the game until the shoe is finished. You are betting $10 on just one hand. (Casinos will let you play two hands. Some will even allow three.) You're dealt two 8's, and the Dealer has a 6 showing, the worst card-up he could have. You immediately split your 8's, placing a second $10 bet next to the second 8. Now you're dealt two more cards—and one is another 8. The other dealt card is a King. You "stand" on your King/8, as you have a playable total of 18. You now split the *third* 8, putting another $10 bet next to it. Again, the Dealer deals you two more cards, one each for the two 8's. You get a 3 and an Ace. Now you have a total of 11 (8 + 3) on one hand, and you "double-down," placing an additional $10 on it. As for the other half of the second split, it now shows a total of 9 *or* 19, Player's choice (remember, the Ace can be 1 or 11). With the dealer showing a 6, you promptly "double-down" again on the 8/Ace hand—you play it now as a total of 9—and place still *another* $10 bet on the cloth next to it.

Okay, time out. Let's rehash that last paragraph and see *exactly* what happened, and what the wagering was, on what started out as an ordinary pair of 8's and one simple $10 bet.

You started with that lone $10 bet. Upon *splitting* the 8's you added a *second* $10 wager, for a total of $20 on the table. Of the two new cards dealt, one was a King, which gave you a comfortable King/8 total of 18, with which you stood. The other card was yet a third 8, which enabled you to split yet again, so you put down another $10 bet. Your bets down now totaled $30.

Two new cards were dealt to you; one was a 3 and the other

an Ace. With an 8/3 count of 11 you doubled-down, and bet still another $10 on the hand. Total bets down now: $40. Here's that last (and controversial) move, your doubling-down on the 8/Ace count—normally a comfortable 19—gambling on the dealer going bust with that deadly 6 as his up-card.

With this last $10 bet you now have parlayed your original $10 wager to an impressive $50—on a table situation where the odds are in *your* favor. Here you have the dealer sitting with the worst possible up-card a blackjack dealer can have.

This is a perfect example of taking advantage of every opportunity you are dealt. The strong odds were in your favor, with the dealer's deadly 6 as his show card. Of course there is no iron-clad guarantee that you would win the hands, but you must always keep in mind that in gambling you always must take full advantage when the odds are in your favor. If you expect to leave the casino with their money, pal, that's the only way you can come out ahead in the long run.

Seed Money

The question people ask me most often is, "How much money should I take with me to the casinos?" I always answer with Gary Cooper's classic reply: "Depends."

Depends on a number of factors. For one, the player's familiarity with casino action. If you're a novice, unsure of yourself and feel uptight at the tables, don't take more than two or three hundred dollars along for the day, and patronize the minimum-bet $5 tables. (Years ago at the "sawdust joints" on Fremont Street in Las Vegas, you could play at $1 and $2 tables.) The logic in all this is that at five bucks a pop you can't really get hurt too bad financially. You won't be wagering "scared money." Scared money *never* wins. I emphasize again that you should only gamble with money that you can comfortably afford to lose, where the loss wouldn't interfere with your lifestyle.

The mistakes you make at the $5 table you'll avoid making when you're wagering at the $25-minimum table or at a $100 table. On-the-job training will serve you well when you play for keeps at higher-limit blackjack.

Even better than starting at the $5 tables, check around the casinos and see whether any of them give free blackjack lessons for beginners.

These free practice sessions are usually scheduled early on weekday afternoons. By all means, take advantage of these freebie excursions to the blackjack tables.

Here you will be able to relax and hone your gambling skills without risking your seed money. Here you can double-down and split cards and generally see how the game goes. (In between these practice sessions you can sidle over to a $5 table to put what you just learned into practice. During such brief "off-campus" forays, limit your goal to a modest $15 win.)

Now you've gotten some free lessons from the casino and you've cut your baby teeth on a few go-arounds at the $5 table. You feel more comfortable and confident with the game of blackjack. So far so good. Now go back to the $5-minimum tables with the firm goal of winning $20 of the casino's money, and quitting winners. That's your *firm* goal, $20. Not $25, not $50, just $20. If you learn self-discipline from the start, it will serve you well throughout your casino career.

I wish somebody had taken me by the hand and given me this sage advice. Oh, how many times have I stayed too long at a table! How many times have I waited around for "just one more hand," "just one more shoe," only to see all my winnings—and sometimes my table stakes—swept away? Remember, just as fast as you won it, that's how fast you can lose it, so pick up your chips and head directly to the cashier's cage, and then right to the exit door, with the casino's $20 in your wallet. It's yours. You won it. As Jackie Gleason phrased it, "How sweet it is. . . ."

Now you're off to the next casino, with your original bankroll of two or three hundred dollars, *plus* your $20 winnings. Now let's see you do it again. This time shoot for twenty-five bucks. Sure, you can do it again; just don't be greedy. Stick to your hit-and-run strategy and, *voila!* you'll now be $45 richer. Keep doing this up and down the Strip, or all along the Boardwalk, and soon you'll be stuffing hundred-dollar bills in your wallet. I can't emphasize enough that having a *specific goal* in mind is essential to quitting as a winner.

Here's a case in point: It was Saturday afternoon in New York. My girl friend at the time was embroiled in a messy and expensive divorce. Her court case was on the docket for Monday. The distraught lady was up a tree financially; she had to come up with $1,600 for her lawyer by Monday morning. Inspired, I grabbed my hat and headed for the door.

"Where are you going?" she asked.

"Off to the Strip, of course. Let's see if I can win some lawyer money for you."

And of course I did. At JFK I took TWA Flight #57 at 5:30 (after all these years, I *still* remember my "usual" flight to Las Vegas!), arriving at the old McCarran Airport at 8:30 Pacific Standard Time. By 8:45 I was at the blackjack tables at the Hacienda. (The Hacienda, along with the Sands, was imploded on national television on New Year's Day, 1996. It had outlived its usefulness. When the new McCarran Airport was built, the road out of the airport ran in the opposite direction. Isolated and alone at the bottom of the Strip, the Hacienda became like Australia prior to the invention of the airplane—everybody knew where it was, but nobody went there.)

But, back in the days when you had to enter Las Vegas by way of the old airport, the Hacienda was the first casino you came to.

In ten minutes I left with $175 of the Hacienda's money, then I hit-and-ran at the Tropicana for another $125. And so it went, all the way down to the Sahara, at which point my total Strip winnings topped $2,200, which more than covered my goal plus expenses. Looking over my scorecard, I never made more than $175 in any one casino. I had a goal and I systematically moved on my goal. I accomplished what I wanted to do by disciplining my table action from the first casino I entered. My lady now had her lawyer money, and her newly-paid attorney creamed her ex-husband in court Monday Morning.

A Tip

Beware of casinos that offer blackjack tables with a $1,000 maximum, *but with a $50 minimum bet*. I have but one thing to say about such tables: Avoid them like the plague! More and more of these rip-off stands are springing up, and they are all one-way tickets to a quick wipe-out.

Dumb Luck

I was at a blackjack table in Caesars Palace, sitting next to a husband who was teaching his wife how to play. New to the game, the lady was confused over the dual value of aces—she didn't understand that they were either valued at one or eleven. So, unwittingly, with a total of 20 she hit—and drew an ace! Her husband, seeing her cards, was understandably furious with her. "But why are you mad at me, honey?" she asked innocently. "I won, didn't I?"

Vegas Vamps

✓ Winning Wanton Women
✓ Catfight With The Sex Kitten:
✓ My Wife Versus Eartha Kitt
✓ Dice With Good Taste

Winning Wanton Women

Make no mistake about it, it took me much too long and a much too painful apprenticeship at the green-felt tables to realize finally that the only way I can beat the casinos is to hit and run.

No longer did I fantasize about cleaning out the cashier's cage. Now I was content to nibble away, and, if I wasn't too greedy and didn't stay too long, I could frequently quit winners and have the fun of the thrill of the chase. As blackjack, and gambling in general, was for me nothing more than a stimulating and challenging avocation—my mail-order book business gave me a comfortable living, thank you—the extra cash, when I won it, was a windfall.

I was a foot-loose bachelor then, so I made a concentrated effort to spend it when I won it. That good-looking painting of Don Quixote in my apartment is a prime example, but my free-wheeling spending habits sometimes took bizarre turns. (I'm happily married now and settled down, but when I think of what I did then, sometimes I shudder.)

A young single guy with a cozy Manhattan apartment and a free dollar didn't have much of a problem attracting chicks, so sex just *wasn't* on my agenda while solo hitting and running in Vegas. I had made it a point to keep my eye on my score card, not on the femmes.

It was sometime in 1973 at a blackjack table at the Sands when it happened. I was alone at the table, except for a lady sitting in the seat right next to mine who, to describe her accurately, looked the epitome of a faded movie star, very elegant and quite striking. I was betting black $100 chips while she was just "nickeling" it, betting $25 chips. In the space between us she had casually put down her Sands hotel key. While the dealer was shuffling for a new round, she deftly pushed the key closer to me, murmuring at the same time in a low stage whisper, "A black chip rents the key."

My initial reaction was negative but, looking closely at her and then down at the key between us, I impulsively pushed a second black chip onto the betting space in front of me. I won the hand and at the same time I won the lady—for a delightful half-hour upstairs.

This was before the Age of AIDS, so henceforth I made it my business to set up a pit stop or two along my casino route. Toward the end of my lecherous side trips I made it a point, whenever possible, to bed down a blonde, a brunette, and a redhead, not necessarily in that order. (The bell captains at many of the Strip and downtown hotels had a hen house full of cuties on hand at all times.) Yes, I readily admit to fucking away some of my casino winnings but here, too, you must agree that there was no way the casinos could ever win it back!

My accountant, along on a Vegas trip with me, was a strait-laced, one-woman man. He envied my Don Juan Vegas adventures, but had no guts to sample the wares. He tagged along, curious to see me in action. During a stop at a downtown casino I excused myself for a black-chip "quickie." Melvin, curious to see what makes a hooker tick, asked me to see if she'd talk to him after our matinee. Once upstairs, I wickedly plotted the seduction of my CPA: I paid her in advance and told the gal if she could actually bed him down, I had *another* black chip for her. The challenge excited *her*, so she was upstairs, lying in wait for Melvin the accountant. Melvin

I guess smelled a rat, and insisted that *she* come down to talk to *him* in the lobby. He never did meet the hooker. The upshot was that the gal got paid, but Melvin didn't get laid.

Catfight with the Sex Kitten: My Wife Versus Eartha Kitt

It was two in the morning at Caesars Palace in Las Vegas. I and Stella—my girl friend at the time—were feeling no pain, fresh out of the opening night, second show, at the Dunes, still rarin' to go. Eartha Kitt was starring in Caesars lounge, so what the hell, for a two-drink minimum we decided it was a perfect way to cap the evening.

It was a midweek night and the lounge was only sparsely filled, so we plopped ourselves down at a ringside table, directly in front of Eartha and her backup quartet. Happy to see a couple of appreciative fans (we really whooped it up, applauding and cheering her every song) she played the show to us. I guess I did have a wee bit too much of the grape under my belt and I was in an alcohol-enhanced playful mood. Otherwise, I wouldn't have dared to do what I did. Wickedly smiling up at Eartha, I lasciviously wiggled my tongue while at the same time rolled my eyes in simulated sexual ecstasy. It immediately caught her attention so, while the backup singers were doing a second chorus of a Cole Porter song, the following dialogue ensued between Stella and the Sex Kitten:

> Eartha (to me): "Come backstage after the show."
> Stella: "You leave my husband alone!"
> Eartha (to me): "Get rid of the broad and meet me backstage."
> Stella (to Eartha): "No such thing! He's coming home with me!"

Me, I was enjoying it all—a famous singer and my girl friend having a nasty cat fight over li'l ol' me. Needless to add, the second the show ended Stella grabbed my arm, held tight, and yanked me out the door and into a cab and back to our hotel.

No, I didn't go backstage, but I can say I ALMOST had a brief fling with a movie star during my daring fantasy life in Las Vegas.

Dice With Good Taste

The most awkward—and most amusing—example of wayward dice that I personally witnessed was at the Desert Inn in Las Vegas, where an overzealous shooter sent one of the dice bouncing off a high roller's stack of chips, after which it flew squarely at the prodigious bosom of the floozie standing across the table from him, and nestled in her cleavage. I'm sure the stickman would have enjoyed retrieving the cube, but the lady deftly reached between her twin peaks and tossed it back onto the table. And—no exceptions—the business-like boxman carefully examined the dice before putting it back into play.

I've read similar accounts in a number of books on gambling. Mamie Van Doren, Jayne Mansfield, Marilyn Monroe—you pick 'em—allegedly had dice popped into their spectacular bosoms. A flavorsome story every time you hear it, but probably just casino folklore.

Then again, the larger the target. . . .

Money

A New Philosophy

How Las Vegas and Atlantic City gave me a whole new philosophy on life and money, and how to spend both wisely . . . *Hot News*, a private book publishing newsletter, recently quoted from a letter written by Nathan Rothschild, founder of the London branch of the Rothschild family: "I don't read books; I don't play cards; I don't go to the theater. My only pleasure is my business."

"That little statement . . . amused me," wrote the editor. "It caused me to reflect on the many wealthy men and women I've known. Most of them had the talent to accumulate large sums of money, but few had another talent: the talent to enjoy it."

The editor was right on target. The quote caused me to reflect on *my* philosophy concerning the role of money in my life; how it ranks in importance, and how I use it. I look back now at how my cash consciousness has radically changed in the past four decades, and the role the casinos played in that change.

Money was green paper that I had earned. I'd spend some and I'd squirrel away some. That was money to me. Then I discovered Las Vegas and the casinos, and suddenly money had a new exciting dimension. I felt much more free in both handling it and spending it.

Whenever I came into a casino windfall, I further honed my spending skills. One of the reasons I got to this mind-set was a comment by casino mogul Bill Harrah. When told that a high roller had just walked out of his casino with a big wad of the casino's cash, Harrah assured his executive, "Don't have to worry, he'll bring it back. I just consider it a temporary casino loan."

Well, with no malice intended, I respectfully say, "Screw you, Mr. Casino Honcho! When I hit it big, I spend it, and you can eat your heart out because you'll never see it again!" With a tight rein on my stop-limit pocket seed money, along with my unwavering no-credit policy, I make sure that I never bring it back. I also make sure that I make use of my winnings, both wisely and frivolously. Recall I even fucked away a nice wad of casino cash during my X-rated days, winning harems of wanton women, all funded by casino money. That they *definitely* can't win back.

I learned the art of buying on impulse with my windfall cash. At times I bought my girl friends expensive presents, often right there in the posh casino shops, and often paying with chips I had just won from the green-felt tables. And on impulse once, flush with casino cash, my girl friend and I flew to exotic Monte Carlo for three mad, exciting days and nights. What a James Bond weekend that was!

I had now learned how to *enjoy* using money. Now I felt so much freer in both buying things and doing things with the winnings. Money—casino money—became fun cash for me. Without this new concept, would I ever have thought of buying a pair of $150 face-value tickets from a scalper on the sidewalk for an outrageous $500 for a once-in-a-lifetime event—*Carnegie Hall Celebrates The Glorious MGM Musicals*! Would Arnold Bruce Levy ever even *THINK* of handing over $500 to a despised sleazy scalper on the sidewalk for a couple of $75 tickets? Not conceivable, that's for sure.

But, I said to myself, whenever again will such a star-studded line-up of legendary movie stars of this magnitude from the Golden Age of Metro-Goldwyn-Mayer ever appear all together on a New York stage? Or, for that matter, on a stage *anywhere* else in the world?

Most probably never.

Walking into the lobby of Carnegie Hall, clutching the much-sought-after tickets, I studied the long line of tired-looking people inside, waiting for hours on the no-ticket line, hoping for ticket cancellations that never came. Some looked very well-to-do, and I'm sure many on that no-ticket line could have bought-and-sold me, and I'd never even know that I was bought-and-sold. As I gazed at those anxious people on the line I knew that I was wealthier and much wiser than *any* of them. I'd put my money to good use, spending it for this once-in-a-lifetime experience that Stella and I cherish in memory forever. Even as I type this, I can still hear the golden echoes of those screen legends singing in person, on stage in magnificent Carnegie Hall, just for *us*!

The $500 for those precious tickets were spent with money I *learned* how to spend through my escapades in the casinos. When I lost there, I only lost what I took with me, and only what I could afford to lose. The $500 for that fabulous evening with my favorites of the silver screen were well-spent with the "fun money" I allowed myself. I am confident that my estate will be no poorer for that extravagant purchase, one that has enriched both Stella's life and mine while we're still here.

Win Big and Play God

One advantage of winning money from a casino is that it's not nine-to-five workaday money. You roll a pair of dice for a couple of hours and suddenly you're hundreds or even thousands of dollars ahead.

My uptight former accountant, who never ever gambled, suggested: "It's time you took a business trip for the calendar year," so I figured what the hell, and took him along with me to Vegas on the way to Los Angeles. A man who never bought a $1 lottery ticket suddenly found himself at a craps table in the middle of a streak.

Melvin didn't know diddly about dice—he was just at the right place at the right time. When he came home with nearly $2,400, his instruction to his equally uptight wife was explicit: "The money isn't to be used for anything practical. We don't buy a couch with it and we don't use it to repaper the kitchen." They finally blew most of it on a weekend cruise to Bermuda—their first ever.

My first adventure in spending "mad money" was at my old Las

Vegas horn of plenty—the Sahara. I had made my usual hit for the day at the Sahara and was on the way to my suite. Along the hallway from the casino to the elevators was displayed exotic and eye-catching oil paintings for sale. I was near the elevators when my roving eye was attracted to a large, dramatic oil painting of Don Quixote on his horse, ready to tilt at the windmill.

It was gorgeous and priced at $500. Now I like art, but I wasn't about to spend $500 of my money even for the Mona Lisa. Sure, I liked Don Quixote, but my art appreciation up to that point had been limited to just looking at paintings on museum and other people's walls.

Impulsively I wheeled around and headed back to the casino. What the hell, I said to myself, let me see if I can win some more of their money to buy the painting. . . .

About a week later the large, well-padded UPS carton arrived at my Manhattan apartment, and for the next few years Don Quixote hung proudly over my couch. My wife is now into theatrical posters, so Don Quixote is currently relegated to a storage space in the spare room. If my workaday money had been in question, you better believe that Don Quixote would still be hanging on the hallway of the Sahara—unless someone else was similarly smitten with it.

♦ ♦ ♦ ♦ ♦

If you really want to, you can even play God with casino winnings. I did it once, and let me tell you right off the bat that I am thoroughly ashamed of what I did. It was an arrogant, discourteous, and almost tyrannical act of mine, and I only relate it here as an example of what *not* to do when you're flying high with casino mad money.

Through our punctuated visits to Las Vegas, Stella and I became friendly with an extraordinary singer named Rouvan, who starred for years as the main attraction of the ongoing "Casino de Paris" shows at the Dunes. He recorded for RCA, and had a voice as good as Mario Lanza's. Rouvan "only" made $25,000 a week during the years when Sinatra made $125,000 and Elvis made $100,000, but as he starred for about twenty-six to thirty weeks-a-year at the Dunes, Rouvan's $25,000 a week totaled to more than the *combined* Las Vegas earnings of Sinatra and Elvis—who each only starred there for a few weeks a year.

A Rouvan opening night at the Dunes was always a perfect excuse for Stella and me to fly to Vegas. This time, however, we didn't make a show reservation. Arriving at the Dunes in plenty of time for the dinner show, we found to our dismay that the showroom was jammed, with a line waiting outside. Haughtily, knowing the power of the $25 green chip, we bucked the line and told the maitre d' we wanted our favorite table, the cozy small one just to the left of the stage. The man looked defeated and forlorn—he'd have to refuse the green chip this time—because two middle-aged ladies already were sitting there.

If it had been my nine-to-five workaday money, or if I had suffered a bad run in the casino on the way in, I would never have dared do what I did. Drawing myself up to my full height of five-foot-eight, and well-juiced with a couple of stiff vodka-and-tonics on the flight in, I thrust a black $100 chip onto the maitre d's palm and dramatically pointed, "We-want-that-table!"

Suddenly the heavens opened and a chorus of angels blared their Golden Trumpets as Arnold Bruce Levy of Brooklyn, New York, played God at the Dunes. The maitre d' had a hurried conversation with the two women, and then escorted them to a table toward the rear of the showroom. Curiously, they were smiling as they left their table. We later found out that the maitre d' used his casino clout and was able to comp the ladies at their table way in the back.

It was, as usual, a spectacular Rouvan opening night, but later I realized what a rude and unsportsmanlike thing I did, which was, for anyone who knows me, totally uncharacteristic.

I ashamedly relate the above episode only to caution you not to ever commit as despicable an act as that. Do what I *say*, not what I *did*. Trust me, you'll never regret *not* doing it.

Sometimes the ham-handed approach doesn't work, anyway. A popular disc jockey in New York once announced over the radio a contest where one lucky listener would win a trip to Las Vegas and be a guest for the Frank Sinatra opening at the Sands. As I listened to his spiel, I decided then-and-there that my girl-friend-of-the-moment would also be a winner, courtesy of me. Arriving in Vegas, I discovered to my horror that the show was sold out. One black chip wouldn't get me anywhere, and definitely not to my "usual" ringside table. Fired up and desperate, I went over to the tables and won $400, which I took to the maitre d'. There were real tears in his eyes as he reluctantly pushed my hand away, explaining that Frank had reserved most of the room for "The Boys."

♠ ♠ ♠ ♠ ♠

Winning a bundle allows you to think like a winner. Three times in my life I missed the last express bus from Atlantic City to Manhattan, and each time I splurged and became The Last of the Big-Time Spenders, taking an Atlantic City taxicab all the way back to New York City, each time at the cost of two black chips. Once I actually did pay the cabby in Trump Plaza black chips.

I already had cashed in $10,000 in chips at the casino, the most you can convert to greenbacks in a twenty-four-hour period in a casino without the nuisance of filling out Internal Revenue Service forms. The remaining chips in my pocket I had planned to use on my next Atlantic City visit, so two of them became convenient cab fare for that night.

Sure, all through this book I've emphasized over and over again that, if you want to beat the dealer and come home with casino money, you shouldn't play big shot and show off for your girl friend. Once I went with my girl friend, a tabloid publisher friend and his wife, along with a mail-order letter-shop owner who had never been west of Hoboken, ALL on a flying weekend to Las Vegas. I postured, I pirouetted, I did wild things at the tables that I would never have done had I been alone.

I gave them a razzle-dazzle round-robin tour of both the Strip and the downtown casinos. I must admit that I felt like James Bond as I made daring bets, some of which, amazingly, paid off. It was just dumb luck that a $57 Keno bet won $605. My recollection is that I only played Keno there to show them all how the game was played. All in all, it was a fast-paced dazzling weekend which I'm sure my little flock will remember always. For me, it was an expensive guided tour, for I was a $3,800 loser. I never made that mistake again and I never will, but what the hell? I guess I got $3,800 worth of fun out of playing "Mr. Vegas" for a weekend.

Mad Money

My then-girl friend Stella, now my wife, also regards my gambling winnings as "found money" to be splurged on fantasies. Of course, when I lost I would explain it was just loose money, the loss of which didn't affect our standard of living, but she still had a few thousand choice words of vituperation for me.

When we were wed, Stella and I spent our honeymoon at the Sahara in Las Vegas—where else? Thinking all good things must come to an end, I found myself standing on the check-out line, feeling good because the Las Vegas tables had paid for our honeymoon. I felt a tap on my shoulder; it was my blushing bride.

"We need a necessity for our apartment."

Warily I asked, "What 'necessity'?"

"A ZEBRA LOUNGE neon sign," she answered, nudging me off the check-out line and pointing me toward the blackjack tables. "You're not finished winning yet," she added.

An explanation is required here.

Our Manhattan apartment has a zebra motif—zebra sheets,

zebra covers, zebra figurines, zebra pictures—zebras everywhere you look. We are up to our ass in zebras.

I shrugged my shoulders, and muttered "what the hell," and headed back into the casino and over to the nearest blackjack table. There, I laboriously ground out another $400 before checking out.

The next afternoon found us at a sign shop in Greenwich Village. We designed a splendid ZEBRA LOUNGE neon sign, which still, as of this very morning, was shining like a beacon over the table as I sipped my breakfast coffee.

Follow my advice: When you win it, go out and spend it! If necessity dictates, then yes, go out and buy that mattress you put off getting because you couldn't afford it. However, if you've got the necessities covered, then dream-that-dream that you dared to dream and make it come true with the "mad money" that you just won! And always remember: If you win it and spend it, the casinos can never win it back. The Sahara Hotel will never ever win back our proud ZEBRA LOUNGE neon sign, that's for sure!

Morey Amsterdam's Investment

Should you ever make a killing at the tables, it's okay to spend it wisely. Morey Amsterdam is mainly remembered as a regular on *The Dick Van Dyke Show*. Amsterdam was also a songwriter (*Rum and Coca-Cola*), and a stand-up comedian in the Vegas lounges in the 1950s and 1960s.

Once, at a Desert Inn craps table, Amsterdam got lucky and won $4,000. "Fat Jack" Leonard, another lounge comedian of the era, knew his friend had a tendency to piss away his winnings, so he convinced him to take the winnings—just this once—and buy some cheap empty land that was for sale some blocks away from the Strip.

In the early 1990s Amsterdam sold the land to a real estate developer for $2.9 million dollars.

Borrowed Money

Money is the real name of the game in the casino.

In 1960, when I first started to gamble in casinos, currency was frequently used as a betting unit in baccarat. Players would put greenbacks on the betting squares and, if they won, the dealer would count out paper money to pay off the bet. $100 chips were top dollar betting units at both blackjack and craps, with higher denomination chips mostly in play at the baccarat table. The cry, "Money plays," with the bettor tossing greenbacks onto the green-felt cloth, was heard frequently in casinos.

I promised you that this book would be anecdotal, so I can't resist telling you about the most unusual loan I ever got. I went along on one of book publisher Lyle Stuart's all-expenses-paid trips to the Sands in Las Vegas for his office crew and friends. As this was during my fledgling years, I was still learning the art and science of wagering, and I was not adroit in either blackjack or craps. The result: My bankroll soon slimmed down to almost nothing. I sometimes tagged along with Lyle on his gambling sprees but, as I was just about tapped out, I explained to my friend that, with the meager funds left at my disposal, I was going to cool it for the rest of the trip and stick with the slot machines. Obviously amused, Lyle led me to the Sands' baccarat table, where he was greeted warmly by the dealers. Lyle stood there, with his hands in his pockets and just stared at the table for a couple of seconds. Then he simply announced, "Two thousand on Player."

That was it. Lyle, just standing there, didn't even take his hands out of his pockets, and of course he didn't put up any money.

"$2,000 on Player for Mr. S," intoned the Caller as the cards were dealt. "The Bank has a natural eight," the Caller announced.

The player at the table with the biggest bet on the Player's side turned his two cards face-up.

"A natural nine for the Player. Player wins, nine over eight. Pay the Player's side."

The dealer counted out twenty-$100 bills and placed them on the cloth. Now, for the first time since we got to the table, Lyle took his hands out of his pockets and reached down to pick up his winnings, which he handed over to me.

"Here, kid, here's a loan. C'mon, let's head over to Caesars. Their baccarat table opens in twenty minutes."

With my newly enhanced bankroll, I resumed my custom of tagging along with Lyle. We went to Caesars and I had my usual exciting time watching my bon vivant friend in action. Did I gamble with Lyle's windfall loan? Not a penny, dear reader. Not a sou. Which brings me to my next rule for you. If you want to be a winner, never—NEVER—gamble with borrowed money. I returned the twenty $100 bills to him as soon as our return flight to New York was in the air.

The Cashier's Cage

Casinos, with all their flash and glitter, might appear to the first-time visitor to be laid out in a somewhat haphazard manner. Nothing could be further from the truth. Casino owners and managers are heavy-hitters, investing Big Bucks in a grim, hard-ball business. You better believe these moguls leave nothing to chance every step of the way, from the positioning of water fountains and restrooms to the location of the cashier's cage, to figuring out where the craps and blackjack tables will be, to the exact aisle space between the rows of the slot machines. (Notice the ample walking space in the rows of the half-dollar and dollar machines, both of which are positioned near the casino entrances.)

♠ ♠ ♠ ♠ ♠

If you hit it big, big enough to cash in at least $5,000 in chips, find out if the casino cashier cage has a side entrance, where there are private booths where you can do your cash transactions away from the milling crowd. There you can request a "certified bundle"—an already-banded pack of fifty-$100 bills, initialed by the tellers. (When my chips count is not quite $5,000, I just add the necessary cash to my pile of chips to receive my neatly-banded certified bundle.) Two casinos in Atlantic City that have the private side entrance are Caesars and the Sands. There are others.

$5,000 Chips

Sounds far-fetched, I know. You've probably never even seen a $5,000 chip, let alone owned one. But here are three horror stories about $5,000 chips, one told to me, one that I witnessed, and one fairly recent episode I read about in a 1999 issue of *Gambling Today*.

The first instance happened on what was supposed to be a jolly and carefree, fun-filled junket to a Caribbean island casino. The husband, who gambled, took along his wife, who didn't. She was just eager to soak up a little winter sunshine.

While strolling through the casino the wife spied a chip on the floor and picked it up. To her amazement and delight it turned out to be a $5,000 chip. Now grandiose thoughts danced in her brain, like how she would surprise her husband with extravagant gifts, etc. Her dream turned into a nightmare when she went to the cashier's cage and tried to cash the $5,000 chip. Immediately the shift boss and the casino manager closed in on her, asking her exactly where she got the chip.

She wasn't a junketeer gambler known to them, and no one had ever seen her at the tables. She told them that she had found it, but that didn't satisfy the casino bosses. Without going into all the nasty by-play, I'll just say that she and her husband fled the island paradise, threatened with arrest! Truth be told, they probably were lucky to get out in one piece.

Another episode concerning a $5,000 chip happened on my watch recently at Caesars in Atlantic City. I was at a $25-minimum blackjack table, as is my wont. Sitting next to me was a young guy, who couldn't have been much older than eighteen, by law the age requirement for gambling in a New Jersey casino.

He pushed a chip toward the dealer for change—a $5,000 chip. The dealer froze and stopped the action. He immediately summoned the pit boss, who asked the kid a few questions and then called over the shift manager. Meanwhile all action at the table stopped.

After the shift manager had interrogated the kid, an impressive casino executive appeared, probably an assistant casino manager. He asked the youth for his ID and then wanted to know where he got the $5,000 chip. Still no action at the table. The lad explained—claimed that his father had given him the $5,000 chip.

After a short sotto-voce conference between the three Caesar stooges, they pushed the chip back to the kid and told him to have his father bring it in. Red-faced and crestfallen, the kid left the table, and at last—the game went forward.

I relate these two $5,000 chip episodes, which occurred thousands of miles apart, to alert you to the perils of accepting high-denomination chips. I wonder what happens to the schnook who stumbles upon a $10,000 or a $25,000 chip.

In 1998 an entirely new set of problems arose over the $5,000 chip, this time in Binion's Horseshoe in Las Vegas. It appears that some very enterprising counterfeiter successfully cloned the casino's $5,000 chocolate chip, panicking the management. Hamid Dastmalchi, winner of the 1992 World Series of Poker, tried to redeem the five-grand chips for $815,000, but was rebuffed at the cashier's cage. The explanation he was given was that, with counterfeit chips in circulation, Binion's would only cash big-money chips they could verify as having been bought or won at the casino.

Gambling Today reported in their January 25, 1999 issue that so far five people have filed complaints about Binion's chip-cashing policies with the Nevada Gaming Control Board. Former casino owner Bob Stupak is among the complainants. Stupak was turned away by the casino's cashiers, so next time he showed up flanked by an impressive entourage of supporters and media in order to put the casino on the spot, and force them to pay up. The result? He was turned away again! An anti-gambling activist to whom Stupak had given one of his chocolate chips also was unable to redeem it for cash.

I read in the Summer 1998 issue of *The Intelligent Gambler* of yet another customer run-in with a casino over the cashing of chips, and again the amount involved was $5,000.

Abdul Jalib, a resident of Las Vegas and a "professional gambler," writes about a friend of his who was playing blackjack at the MGM Grand casino for several days, losing steadily. At last his luck turned, and slowly but surely he hacked away so that finally he was even. At the cashier's cage he was asked where he won the money, and he explained that he won it little by little at tables all across the casino. The MGM Grand is a large place, with lots of blackjack tables, making his story entirely plausible —even common.

Incredibly, the cashier refused to cash his $5,000 in chips, and after a hassle she begrudgingly agreed to cash $2,500's worth. When he took the other $2,500 in chips to another cashier, the first cashier rushed over, screaming, "Don't cash those chips!" Only after the player went to see the casino manager and bitterly complained was he finally able to redeem the rest of his chips. Needless to say, he informed the manager in no uncertain terms that he would never ever again patronize the MGM Grand.

If it should happen to me, neither would I. And neither should you. If any casino becomes a hassle, avoid it and gamble elsewhere.

High Rollers and Whales

There is a small clique of gamblers in a class by themselves. They aren't like you and I. They number a scant few hundred, but they are the real meat-and-potatoes of big casino action. The gamblers I'm talking about make the fabled Nick the Greek look like a penny-ante player.

The majority of them are Asians who fly in on chartered jets with a retinue of bodyguards, mistresses, cooks, and interpreters. Whole baccarat pits are reserved just for them and are often specially redecorated to suit the tastes of these Very Special Players.

Casinos will go to extraordinary lengths to attract them. They wager in huge sums, and their limits at the tables can reach mind-boggling numbers. They are referred to in casino inner-circles as "whales."

Akio Kashiwagi was a whale. Baccarat was his game. According to a feature story in *The National Enquirer*, this High Roller literally broke the bank when he raked in $22 million from an Australian casino, and then followed up by winning *another* $12.2 million from one of Donald Trump's casinos. Trump successfully lured him into returning, and his casino was able to win back $10 million of it. But that didn't faze this Japanese jetter—he still had $24 million left in winnings when the smoke cleared.

Kashiwagi often brought $10 million as seed money, gambling for as long as fourteen hours a day. He took his gambling seriously, turning a large part of his mansion in Japan into a miniature casino, complete with baccarat table, dealer—even a cocktail waitress! When at home, he practiced ten-hours-a-day just "to keep in shape."

Kashiwagi was a wheeler-dealer in Japanese real estate, operating on the fringe of legitimacy. Finally his luck ran out, not at the tables but with his real estate dealings. When his house of cards collapsed, Kashiwagi committed suicide.

Kerry Packer, Australia's wealthiest man, is another whale who gambles for gigantic sums. He stuck it to Steve Wynn when he won a hefty six million bucks from his prize casino, the Mirage. His *coup de grace* occurred in 1996 when, in less then two hours, he beat the Las Vegas MGM Grand for almost $24 million. This adventurous Aussie—a casino owner himself in his native Australia—was betting as much as a quarter-of-a-million dollars *a hand!*

Though normally a casino owner will do just about anything in the world to coax a whale into his casino, MGM Grand owner Kirk Kerkorian flew a personal representative to Australia just to tell Packer face-to-face that his business was no longer welcome at the MGM Grand. Casino old-timers say this is the first time in living memory anything like this ever happened.

♠ ♠ ♠ ♠ ♠

The highest-stakes game I ever witnessed was a chemin de fer session in 1964 at Crockford's Casino in London, with auto magnate Henry Ford II, movie producer Otto Preminger, and an Arab sheik at the table. London chips get bigger as their value increases, and the chips I saw going back and forth across the table were HUGE.

♠ ♠ ♠ ♠ ♠

Only one time in all my casino cruising have I ever seen a craps table run out of chips. It was in the 1960s at the Sands. The table was elbow-to-elbow with High Rollers, all from Providence, Rhode Island. The table minimum was $100, a rarity in the 1960s.

Lady Luck really smiled on the enthusiastic Rhode Islanders as the black chips rapidly disappeared from in front of the boxmen, streaming across the table to the red-hot Providence crowd. To my astonishment, security men suddenly showed up with a rolling table, piled high with racks of the old, discontinued black chips of the 1950s—the cute ones with the smiling cowgirl and the logo, "Come As You Are." It was nice seeing them again.

Money Doesn't Play in Atlantic City

When I first went to Vegas in the 1960s, it was a free-and-easy town. The casinos, as a rule, were small and friendly. The $100 chip was usually the top denomination in play at the tables, so it was standard procedure for a player to have a wooden rack close at hand to keep his chips in. A player could walk over to a black-jack table, drop greenbacks on the felt, and tell the dealer, "Money plays." When the player won, he would pick up his bills, put them in his pocket and gamble with the chips he won.

Not in Atlantic City, pal! The first time I placed my greenbacks on the table for a bet, the dealer swiftly gathered them up and zipped them into the drop box, exchanging my money for chips.

Annoyed, I wrote it off as petty bullshit. But as time went by, it dawned on me how clever and sophisticated the marketing geniuses in the casino front offices had become. Now follow me on this: When you play for money, real greenback folding money, you're more aware, more cautious. You're looking down on cash you made by the sweat of your brow. But once the dealer exchanges it for the casino's multicolored chips, it suddenly ceases to be "real" money. Now you're playing with play money.

If you stand back a little and put it all in perspective, the pieces fit neatly into place. The player (read that as "patsy") is in a con-trolled atmosphere where Father Time is an absentee dad. A place with no windows and no clocks, a place where low, soothing lights and music in the background puts the player in a perpetual Twilight Zone. Like Pinocchio on Pleasure Island, he is a kid again, able to have all his whims satisfied: free cigarettes and drinks served by half-naked *Playboy* centerfold-type waitresses at his beck-and-call (you never see a guy serving drinks).

As for the chips, he often bets them without restraint. And why not? They're "only" chips, not the *real* money he barters in a work-a-day world. The dealers help feed the myth of make-believe for the player with their unique terminology: You're not betting $25—you're betting "a quarter." You're not betting five real dollars—you're betting "a nickel." You can begin to see how easy it is for the casino to lull the player into losing a sense of reality.

If you think all this is just applesauce, just think back on the times you were flying high at the table, a fortune in the casino's chips in front of you. A shoe or two later—wham!—the tide turned in the casino's favor, as it eventually always does, and you were soon tapped out.

If you weren't so zonked and brainwashed by the casino's controlled environment, you probably would have grabbed your chips while the going was good and headed directly to the cashier's cage.

I know of what I write. I was the patsy too many times in the situations discussed above. Oh, how many times I had it, but greed consumed me and I stuck around for "just one more shoe." And, dammit, how many times I lost it all!

So don't be an ass like I used to be. Don't get lured into the "casino trance," where you lose track of your table/casino goal and get swallowed up in Pinocchio's Pleasure Island syndrome. When you reach your predetermined goal, run out of the casino with your winnings. Don't join me and Pinocchio in the donkey house.

Comps

There are actually books on gambling that'll give you tips and secrets for getting complimentary meals, lodgings, and shows, all courtesy of your friendly casino. Ditto the many junkets you can sign up for to casinos everywhere.

With a couple of exceptions, I have passed on 'em all. No thank you. I've done this for several reasons, but primary among them is that I don't want my gambling monitored. Being "rated" is the term they use at the tables, the translation of which is that the pit boss is feeding a computer on how much you're betting, how often you're betting, and exactly how you're doing.

I don't care how much of a cool cat you are, or how much you insist that it won't affect your play. It will! When you're concentrating on your action you need to focus 100 percent on what you're doing. You shouldn't be looking over your shoulder at the pit boss, wondering, "Am I 'rated' enough to get us comped at the show tonight?" Frankly, pal, if you're betting green or black chips at the table, just a couple of wins in even one or two hands will be enough dough for you and your wife to handsomely "toke" the maitre d' for ringside in the showroom, and that way you'll be your own man at the tables.

Outside of the run I had at the Sahara, where the casino executive handed me a suite on an open-end basis, I've passed on the comps. I did, just once in the mid-1970s, accept a casino's offer of a gambling weekend at Lake Tahoe. It was an offer that I just couldn't refuse. Checking my mail at home, I found a tall and impressively ornate special delivery package awaiting me, hand-addressed in the manner of a scribe of old to "Sir Arnold of Levy."

Intrigued, I opened it and found a parchment proclamation, announcing that Sir Nathan of Jacobson would like to have the Extreme Honor & Pleasure of the presence of the (aforementioned) Sir Arnold of Levy and His Lady at the gala opening of Kings Castle Casino at Lake Tahoe, Nevada.

What really got my attention was that the Proclamation said our first-class round-trip air fare would be paid. I was sold, and off to Reno we went. (No airports in Tahoe back then.)

Arriving at Reno, we found that the only way to get to Kings Castle was by cab over the mountain roads. Frankly, except for my two years in Korea during the war, I was never so scared in my life as traversing those narrow and treacherous lanes. When we checked in, we had to cool our heels outside our room; the carpenters were still inside hammering away.

We couldn't even go to the casino to play a few hands of blackjack or even play the slots; Kings Castle's gambling license wasn't valid until the next day.

Tuckered out from the long plane ride and hazardous trip across the mountains, we were happy just to finally hit the sack. Sleeping soundly, we were jolted awake at 6:00 A.M. by the incessant ringing of a fire alarm. The lame excuse we got later was that they had to test it, but I suspect the real reason was to get the hotel full of freeloaders out of the sack and into the casino so they could start to get a return on their investment.

In the casino I gazed upon as many movie stars as I've ever seen in one place. Present were Lana Turner, Ray Bolger, Barbara Stanwyck, Edward G. Robinson, Jack Benny, and many more. But it wasn't Lana Turner or Ray Bolger . . . it was Lady Lana of Turner and Sir Ray of Bolger. Some of the pagings were quaint and some rather comical: Sir Pat of Kelly, Sir Abe of Cohen, Sir Groucho of Marx.

The weekend was colorful and diverting, but gambling-wise nothing to write home about. The real excitement for me was the three months of Indian wrestling I had to go through—including letters to both the Nevada Governor and the Casino Control Commission—before I was reimbursed for our first-class air fare. So, as a general rule, be your own person and resist all the tempting comps proffered. When you walk away from the tables a winner on your own terms, you'll be happy you followed my advice and kept your gambling independence.

Chip Collecting

Through the four decades of my casino hopping I accumulated a box full of casino chips from all over the world. Visiting Monte Carlo and London, I made it my business to save a chip or two for souvenirs. In Virginia City, Nevada, I couldn't resist the colorful $5 chip used in the Bucket of Blood Saloon casino. When I won a couple hundred dollars there, I took my winnings all in their $5 chips to use for presents. Frankly, from other casinos I just accumulated them, and never gave them a second thought. Then, opening up my Sunday *News* of October 18, 1998, to my astonishment, there blazing across the front page of the Fall Casino Guide, was IN THE CHIPS: THE COLLECTING CRAZE THAT'S PAYING OUT.

The full-page feature article inside told of the fast-growing 2,000 strong National Casino Chip & Gaming Token Collectors Club (P.O. Box 63, Brick NJ 08923) that had a website and holds an annual convention in Las Vegas.

"Collecting chips has a *plus* factor that most other collectibles do not have," said Archie Black, president of the club. "Whenever you want to cash in your chips you can at face value." And if the casino no longer exists, your chips will be a hot property and of considerable interest to collectors.

A $100 chip from the Flamingo of 1946 and 1947, when Bugsy Siegel ran the joint, recently sold for $3,500, and even a $100 chip from the Brighton Casino (now the Sands) in Atlantic City sells for thousands of dollars today.

Now how should you start your collection? My suggestion is to save a couple of $1 chips from each casino where you win. If the casino has 25¢ chips, you can become The Last of the Big-Time Spenders as you pocket a half-dozen of them. (I even have some 10¢ chips from the "sawdust joints" of downtown Vegas that catered to Low Rollers in the 1960s and '70s.)

If you made a nice score at certain casinos you might even save a $5 chip or two from there. If you're not a High Roller I urge you not to save any $25 or $100 chips—yet.

A Few Words on How Money Changes People

A Las Vegas cab driver related the following story while taking me from the downtown Four Queens up to Caesars Palace on the Strip. A couple of high school sweethearts in Encino, California, got engaged and planned to marry right after graduation. Something happened between them and they broke up, each eventually marrying someone else.

Twenty years passed. The fellow was a widower now and he was a city bus driver in Las Vegas. On a regular run, he chanced to overhear a conversation between two women sitting directly behind him. They were discussing a mutual friend, and he suddenly realized that they were talking about his old flame. He questioned them and was delighted to learn that she was also now a resident of Las Vegas, and recently widowed.

Of course, he promptly looked her up. Sparks flew and the flame rekindled, as they picked up where they had left off two decades before in high school. Once again, they made plans to get married.

Stopping for a drink at the then newly opened Four Queens, the fellow filled out two sweepstake tickets for a $500,000 prize. The tickets had been dropped off by the waitress along with their drinks, an opening- month promotion for the new casino. As a gesture of his devotion and love, he put his betrothed's name on both tickets.

Of course she won the half-million. And the first thing she did was dump the bus driver.

Cheating

✓ A Two-Way Street

✓ Case-in-Point

✓ The Gambler Strikes Back, Part I

✓ Card Counting

✓ Illegal Casinos

✓ Anatomy of a Casino Promotion, or How I Got Bamboozled

Cheating Two-Way Street

Does cheating go on in the casinos? You're goddam right it does—by both the dealers and the players.

From the 1940s through the early 1960s, when the mob ran the Las Vegas casinos, often there would be a High Roller who was running a little too lucky at blackjack and apparently was on his way to breaking the bank. Then the casino would bring in a "mechanic"—a cardshark who could control the hand-held deck and grind the hotshot down to size. Today, with most casinos using shoes with multiple decks of cards, it is difficult—but not impossible—to scam the players. More about that later.

Do players cheat the casino? You're damn right they do. In most cases, however, they need the help of dishonest casino employees to pull off their scams. In the old days, if a dealer was tipped off that there were no "Eye in the Sky"—security men on catwalks peering down on the action with telescopic lenses—he might pay off an accomplice/player on every hand, no matter what the cards totaled. Later they'd get together and split the take. Today they have high-fidelity video cameras in operation all the time, and trained on most (but apparently not all) of the tables.

Let me tell you some personal experiences.

During the 1960s on the graveyard shift—the post-midnight hours—I was at the Horseshoe in downtown Vegas shooting craps. It was just me and another player, I at one end of the table, the shooter at the other end. The point was 6. I was playing the Pass Line with a black chip, backing up my bet all the way. The shooter shot wildly, sending one of the cubes spinning off into that little dark corner on the side of the dice box. The die on the table was a 3. The other die, out of sight of everyone except the stickman and me, was a 4, for a total of 7, a loser.

"Hard 6, pay the line," intoned the stickman as he deftly scooped up the out-of-sight die and put it back into play. As fast as I was paid off, that's how fast I hightailed it out of the casino. Evidently the stickman knew that no Eye-in-the-Sky was monitoring the table, or perhaps he was in cahoots with the security man on the catwalk and he was trying to enlist me in the scam for a series of hefty tips. Either way, I wanted no part of it. Scamming casinos isn't my style, and going into business with dishonest stickmen isn't for me either.

That wasn't the only time I was approached on a scam. I was sitting alone at the Sahara's casino bar on the Strip, nursing a beer, when a stranger took the stool next to me.

"You don't know me, but I know you," he began. "I'm a blackjack dealer on the graveyard shift at the Four Queens downtown and I've had you in action at my table. You look like a savvy guy who's with it, so maybe we can make some extra bucks together." I listened as he went on to outline a plan for us to work together on a 50-50 basis. He said he knew exactly when the Eye-in-the-Sky wasn't in operation. Before he could elaborate on his plan, I gulped the rest of my beer and started for the men's room.

"Thanks, but rip-offs aren't my bag," were my parting words to him.

Yes, it appeared that some blackjack dealers knew when the

catwalks were unmonitored. I was once at the Desert Inn playing open blackjack. The dealer was a whizz—man, was he fast! The cards were skillfully snapped off the top of the decks (it was a hand-held two-deck game.) The cards and his hands went faster and faster. Not a rapid calculator, I had the feeling that the five or six little cards I was dealt totaled more than 21, but he paid me and swiftly swept the cards away. Now I was alerted, and damned if the next string of small cards he put in front of me didn't total 22, and yet I was paid again!

Maybe I did the wrong thing, but for one of only two times in my life I tipped the dealer before leaving the table. I threw the bastard a bone because it goes against my nature to get something for nothing. But it was most uncomfortable for me to be the unwitting "winner," boxed into being an accomplice!

A big-time baccarat scam was perpetrated on the Atlantic City casinos a few years back. A planeload of whales from Hong Kong descended on the town and in a series of lightning moves shot from casino-to-casino, making major killings at the baccarat tables.

It was their version of Hit and Run. Once they had their bounty, they got back on the plane to Hong Kong. Wags joked that it was surprising the plane could get off the ground, it was so loaded down with casino money.

The casinos were stunned. They knew something was wrong, but they couldn't put their finger on it. They went back and played and replayed the videotapes of the Asian contingent in action. The first thing they noticed was that at every casino just one of the Chinese players seemed to be the "lucky" one, and when he got the shoe, all the other players would bet heavily with him.

Finally, after endless rerunning of the videotapes someone noticed something—an unusual hand motion used by the "lucky" player with the shoe. As far as I know that's as far as the casino people got in their investigations, and I haven't heard that they ever got any money back.

In one of John Scarne's classic books on casino gambling, he relates an episode at the baccarat table in the Mafia-run Sevilla Baltimore in pre-Castro Havana. The mobster/owners scoffed at Scarne's claim that a player could cheat the casino in baccarat. Scarne bet $500 that he could do it, and with all the boys watching. Scarne asked for—and got—$10,000 in chips for the purpose of testing his boast.

The game commenced. The dealer dealt a few $100 hands before Scarne announced a $10,000 bet on the next hand (which was not unusual in 1958 Havana). Scarne reached for the two cards, held them face down for a few beats, then neatly turned them over, showing a 9 and a picture card—a natural 9.

The dealer paid off the bet and dropped the cards into the discard slot with his shovel. Before the next hand could be dealt, Scarne stopped the game. He asked the dealer to retrieve the discards from the previous hand. The cards were fished out of the pail, and to the casino owners' astonishment and dismay they discovered that in between the standard Bicycle-backed casino cards were two different-backed cards that Scarne had switched into the game!

In his definitive book *On Baccarat*, Lyle Stuart relates how a baccarat shoe was stacked right in front of his eyes. After much shuffling and cutting, the dealer orchestrated a run of baccarat hands for Stuart, telling him in advance exactly what the hand would be! Even when being dealt baccarat, be alert at all times.

With the computer age, cheating has become sophisticated and high-tech. This was brought to public attention in October of 1998, when the New York *Daily News* reported that Jorge Torres of Las Vegas was arrested at Bally's Park Place Casino in Atlantic City after playing at a Caribbean Stud Poker table. New to American casinos, Caribbean Stud isn't a new card game at all; it was introduced long ago on cruise ships that visited the islands. Although it's called poker, it is played only against the dealer, not against other players. It features a progressive jackpot that can reach $300,000 or more.

As the official complaint charged, Torres was arrested "for using cheating techniques." Exactly how he was allegedly beating the house the police refused to say, "because the investigation is ongoing," but the cops confiscated a micro-mini camera that Torres had tucked into his jacket sleeve.

Inside his pickup truck in the casino parking lot were a satellite dish, transmitting equipment, and monitors. Police sources speculated that the suspect was actually just testing the equipment for later use by his Las Vegas gang that had already hit a number of Nevada casinos.

♠ ♠ ♠ ♠ ♠

Lyle Stuart said it best in one of his invaluable books on gambling: To entice a "whale" into a casino, the casino would supply him with baked human being if that was what he wanted. Of course, Lyle was being facetious, but his point was well taken. Not just for whales though—the casinos will go to all lengths to rope in players.

To entice Asian High Rollers, one Strip casino imported an entire Chinese opera company to perform in their show room— just to lure this small segment of players into their casino.

Casinos will go to great lengths to corral a gambler and his or her bankroll. They sponsor the endless line of subsidized buses (mostly filled with slot-machine-addicted women), and chartering jets all the way from Hong Kong and Tokyo to bring in whales.

With new casinos opening in so many states, the casinos in Puerto Rico are hurting.

A friend recently showed me his invitation to a Puerto Rican junket. The invitation offered not just a comped round-trip airfare, but also included a non-transferable $500 chip as a bonus. When they run out of freebies and comps, they now bait the velvet-lined trap with money!

The cleverness and ingenuity of casino promotion people, and the fantastic lengths they'll reach to lure gamblers into their lairs, never ceases to amaze me.

A gimmick employed by the Lady Luck Casino in Vegas during the summer of 1998 was damn clever. They mounted a spectacular show featuring a famous magician and a line of chorus girls, all backed by elaborate, flashy sets.

A patron could come and see the razzle-dazzle show for free—that's right, for free. Well, almost for free. The patron had to first make a detour into the casino and place just one $50 bet on the blackjack table. Win, lose, or push—*voila!*—you've earned your free ticket.

If you won the bet, you got to see the show for free, with fifty bucks of the casino's money in your pocket to boot. If you lost the bet, the show would only cost you $19, as the going price for a ticket was $69.

A "push" would get you your free ticket, with no money changing hands.

The casino's agenda was simply to get you to their $50 blackjack table. I would wager that very few of the prospective showgoers had ever placed fifty bucks at one time on one bet before. The casino bosses were, of course, hoping the player would stick around and play more than that one required hand.

♠ ♠ ♠ ♠ ♠

Shills—people hired by the casino to look like gamblers and start up table games—are commonly used in Nevada casinos. New Jersey law forbids the practice, so you'll find no shills in Atlantic City.

♠ ♠ ♠ ♠ ♠

More than once during a casino visit to Las Vegas I was priv-ileged to be escorted up to the catwalk over the casino tables—the ever-vigilant "Eye in the Sky." Here, security people were able to study both the table games and the banks of slot machines below with powerful telescopes that could read the spots on the cards. Except that, during the times I was up on the catwalk, I didn't ever once see a real live person manning a telescope! I guess the FEAR of someone up there looking down on the tables was enough to keep both the dealers and the crooked patrons in line. Today, the catwalks and the telescopes are gone, replaced by video cameras focused on the tables.

♠ ♠ ♠ ♠ ♠

Don't get greedy. That's a good rule for you and it also goes for a gang of high-tech crooks armed with computer chips who ripped off Vegas slots for millions of dollars. Their downfall came in July, 1988, when they were caught red-handed plotting to rip off the $17 million Megabucks. They didn't remember that the pig ends up in the slaughterhouse.

♠ ♠ ♠ ♠ ♠

I always thought it was rather stupid of the casinos to engage magicians demonstrating clever card tricks in their showrooms. Gamblers exit the showrooms and pour directly into the casinos, coming face-to-face with blackjack dealers and their hand-held decks. Seeing skillful magicians like Arnold "Doc" Boston in action with a deck of cards should convince you to play blackjack shoe games exclusively.

♠ ♠ ♠ ♠ ♠

Often in Las Vegas, as in life, things aren't what they seem to be. During the days when casino chips were interchangeable, and every casino would take each other's chips, a downtown casino came up with an impressive-looking new 25¢ chip. It was a bright green, and in fact looked *so impressive* that some Strip casinos unwittingly paid them off, when played, as "quarters" ($25 chips). The word got around quickly when a dealer at a craps table took a real good look at one of them. . . .

♠ ♠ ♠ ♠ ♠

Sometimes you can't tell the good guys from the bad guys in Nevada. The July 20, 1998 issue of the *New York Post* reported that former Gambling Control Board Agent Ron Harris was arrested for rigging slot machines. He was sentenced to seven years in state prison.

♠ ♠ ♠ ♠ ♠

During one trip to Atlantic City, I paused at a roped-off bank of $5 slot machines. A typical cleaning-lady type—I don't know any other way to describe her—was pumping two $5 tokens, in tandem, into each of two $5 machines simultaneously, and at breakneck speed! I calculated the fast money she was pumping into the two machines was definitely enough to classify her as a Slot Machine High Roller. A player betting a black chip or two at a blackjack table in the baccarat pit couldn't match the rapid-fire four-coin totals she was feeding the two machines in an identical time span.

The reckless abandonment with which she was feeding her huge pile of $5 tokens into the machines led me to believe that she must be some sort of minor civil service functionary, probably from New York City, who had stumbled onto a crack in the proverbial floorboards where she could siphon off governmental money without getting caught. This was all speculation, of course, but I couldn't help speculating.

You know what I'm talking about. Every now and then you read about the civil servant who managed to funnel some city or state funds through loose controls. Like the parking metermaid who discovered a complete set of keys for all the parking meters in Manhattan. She systematically emptied as many of the meters as she could during her off-hours. When the authorities finally caught her, they found 29,000 quarters in a row of cans lined up in the back of her minivan. She was all ready for—you guessed it—her regular weekly run to Atlantic City, where she turned the quarters into folding money at casino coin cashiers' booths.

♠ ♠ ♠ ♠ ♠

Don't let anyone tell you that the Megabucks slots are rigged and "timed" so that the jackpots are electronically spaced out and can be hit only at certain intervals. That lie was put to rest on Sunday, October 23, 1994 at Caesars in Atlantic City. At 2:30 in the afternoon a couple hit the Quartermania for $1.5 million. Six hours later a guy walked over to the same bank of slot machines and hit the Quartermania again—this time for $407,505.

♠ ♠ ♠ ♠ ♠

I've shown how rogue dealers can cheat players and how players (usually in cahoots with dishonest dealers) can cheat casinos. But wait—there's more (or less). Casino cashiers can give you a "fast count." Be on the alert when cashing in your chips, and don't get shorted.

Finally, casinos—in the person of pit bosses and casino executives—can steal money directly from their patrons. This isn't hearsay or suspicion. I know. I was cheated. My chips were stolen from me right before my eyes. I'll not bandy words. Two casino executives screwed me for the benefit of the goddam casino, and they did it brazenly, right in front me, apparently with no fear of being nailed by the Eye in the Sky videotaping mandated by the Casino Control Commission. The following section is devoted to this episode, which I hope will serve as a warning to you.

Case-in-Point

Sure, I like to win the casinos' money, but I only want to win it honestly. It's my way of life; I'm an ethical fellow. I only wish that the Atlantic City casino employees who brazenly stole my chips right off the blackjack table shared my philosophy.

You would think, considering the incalculable value of a gambling license, that the casino executives who walk around with painted smiles, patting their lollipops on the back, wouldn't jeopardize losing their precious certification over a cheap nickel-and-dime swindle. But they swindled me.

Come to think of it, how many times in the past have you and I read of casinos being fined heavily for money laundering, entertaining known mobsters who had been forbidden casino entrance, or honeying up to minors who somehow got their young hands on a chunk of the family fortune and brainlessly blew it all at their tables? And how about the cases where the casino panics when a player has a lucky streak, and pulls a fast one by arbitrarily lowering the maximum at the table in defiance of the strict Casino Control Commission rule requiring the posting of a written notice of a change in the table limit?

The Tropicana Casino in Atlantic City tried to pull this on Anthony Campione of Mays Landing, New Jersey in 1989, as reported in *The New Jersey Law Journal and The New York Times*. In the middle of Campione's winning streak the nervous casino honchos panicked and, in direct violation of the rules, suddenly and arbitrarily, cut the maximum bet at the table from $1,000 to $100. Shocked and appalled, Campione put his hand over the cards—

which stopped the game—and asked to speak to a manager.

Instead of a casino executive, burly security guards showed up and arrested him, accusing Campione of violating Casino Commission regulations governing "conduct in a casino."

Arraigned and eventually put on trial, Campione was acquitted of the trumped-up charges. Once cleared, he promptly sued the Tropicana Hotel and Casino for false arrest and harassment. A Camden County jury awarded Mr. Campione $1,475,500, which included the jury's estimate of $300,000 he *would* have won had he been permitted to keep betting at the $1,000 limit.

Slot machines are, dollar-for-dollar, the sweetest moneymakers for casinos. They're also the surest. I once heard a matronly lady ask a Caesars Palace casino executive, "Do these machines pay?"

"You bet they pay, lady," was his candid reply. "They pay our rent, overhead, electric bill. . . ."

Some greedy casino operators were recently exposed by the newspapers for perpetrating this latest slot scam: When a progressive slot machine gets really top-heavy with a hefty jackpot, these exploiters of the human condition simply remove it from the casino floor! And the courts have upheld them!

Now do you still believe that the friendly casino hosts with the broad smiles and the friendly pats on the back are rooting for you to win any of the casino's money? No, I didn't think you did. . . .

Even when they win their money, they'll put obstacles in your path to the cashier's cage. Once at the Claridge, which bills itself as "The Friendliest Casino in Atlantic City," I won a couple of thousand, but it was all in black and green ($100 and $25 chips). When I asked for them to "color me up" (change my chips to purple $500 chips) so they'd be easy to carry to the cashier's cage, the pit boss, who had been glowering at me throughout my winning streak, now strutted over to the table and demanded that I "show identification" before he'd change color.

I normally keep a low profile at the tables, but this was just too much for me. I reared up and bellowed, "Just to 'change color' you want MY identification? MISTER, THIS IS AN OUTRAGE! I'M GOING TO THE CASINO CONTROL COMMISSION ON THE FLOOR! LET ME SEE *YOUR* IDENTIFICATION! LET ME SEE YOUR BADGE!" (All Atlantic City casinos have a Casino Control Commission office on the casino floor.)

The son of a bitch, now intimidated, started to back away. I made a show of it as I copied his name onto a napkin. Of course I got my change of color, and of course I did nothing in regard to the nasty pit boss. Like I said, I keep a low profile. I wasn't looking for trouble.

And now for the story I promised at last chapter's end.

I never expected a major casino to go to the extreme lengths of risking their casino license just to steal money from me, and right off the blackjack table!

Maybe they knew something—perhaps a lapse in video surveillance at my table. Maybe they took me for a hick from the sticks who didn't know his way around a casino. Maybe I rankled them just enough with my almost systematic whittling away at their casino that they became so infuriated that they just didn't give a damn, and wanted to scare me away from their casino. It could have been any one of the above; maybe it was none of the above. The only thing I am certain of is that between $1,500 and $1,800 was stolen from me by a couple of casino executives, right in front of me, as I sat at a $100 minimum table in their baccarat pit.

A few years back, I would take a day off a week—sometimes even two days off if I had a good outing earlier in the week—and bus it into Atlantic City for five hours of "hit and run." I'd take the first bus (7:00 A.M.) to the seashore, which got me there by 9:30.

By 9:45 I'd be at the tables, hopefully chipping away at the casinos one-by-one, a coupla hundred here, a coupla hundred there. (Oh sure, there were weeks when I lost my seed money and dragassed home early like a beaten dog.) By 2:45 I'd taxi to the old Atlantic City bus terminal, which has since been razed, in time to catch the 3:00 P.M. bus to New York, which would bring me home by 5:30 P.M.

Five hours traveling, five hours in the casinos. A perfect day at the seashore. I guess after a while the pit bosses and casino executives had me spotted as a weekday afternoon "hitman" at their blackjack tables.

That fateful Thursday afternoon I wandered into the baccarat pit of—no, in fairness I won't name the casino, as it has since changed hands. This particular casino, like my old reliable Sahara in Las Vegas, was my personal "Gong"—I hit it rather regularly. Usually it would be for only a couple hundred; sometimes half-a-grand. Sure, many times I'd lose it all at the next casino on my itinerary, but that particular casino for some reason was usually a pay-off place for me. I suppose the honchos were tearing their hair out in frustration over my frequent winning forays.

It was rather late for me that particular Thursday afternoon, a little after 2:00. My Gong casino was going to be my last stop for the day; I had already hit it earlier that day for $175 as my first "call," right off the bus. This was my second visit to the seashore that week; I was there Tuesday and did well, especially at my old faithful Gong casino.

Surveying the floor, I wandered into the baccarat pit. There were a couple of $50 minimum blackjack tables in operation; one was nearly packed, while the other had two smokers playing. I don't play at tables with smokers because I don't play with losers, and smokers are losers. In the rear was an empty $100 minimum table. I opted for the back table. I started my play and, this being the Gong casino, I found myself on a streak. After a bit, I noticed that the lady dealer was peering over my shoulder and looking agitated. She then started to speed up the play. As I was winning, I played right along with the gag, quipping about her sudden burst of energy with the cards. Finally, at the end of the shoe I pushed in my piles of chips and told her, "Change of color, please."

Now I'm going to take it s-l-o-w-l-y in describing exactly what happened next. Very suddenly—from out of nowhere—a man appeared to my left; there he was, a smiling, fast-talking thirtyish casino executive. He moved so close to me that I could feel his hot breath on my cheek. He thrust his "glad hand" in front of me, all the time talking nonstop, proffering some kind of casino comp. With his sudden "friendly" intrusion and his extended hand, *instinctively* and civilly I turned my face toward him and extended my own hand.

At this moment, from the corner of my eye I saw an older, heavyset man in the pit—he, too, materialized out of nowhere—elbowing the lady dealer aside. With the deft hands of an old-time "sawdust" casino pro, he deftly changed my chip colors for me. By this time, Smiley, to my left had finished his breathless canned promo, which had been delivered in one long run-on sentence. The heavyset man in the pit had vanished as fast as he had appeared.

The smiling man then rose, continuing his mile-a-minute spiel, while rapidly backing away. In a moment he had disappeared into the casino crowd. It didn't dawn on me until later that this effusive, overeager casino executive, who so gushingly offered to lavishly comp me, never offered his card, a *de rigueur* ritual of casino hosts.

The total time elapsed for the above little drama probably didn't exceed thirty seconds.

Now I took stock of my chips. The heavyset older man had changed more than my colors—he also changed the amount. As I played, I always kept a rough running total of what I was winning, how far I was ahead. Since my philosophy of gambling is not to be greedy, I make it a point to never, but never, try to win more than my table stakes. This time my table stakes were $2,000, and

I figured I had more than double that in chips, for a sensational $2,000 or $2,500 hit, one of my biggest ever there.

Now I looked at my chips, and then up at the lady dealer. Rarely have I seen a more conflicted, guilty, pained expression on a person's face; she seemed ready to collapse.

I counted the chips in front of me. There was my $2,000 seed money, but instead of my $2,000 to $2,500 in winnings I counted only $1,050. The heavyset man had repossessed half my winnings or more for the Gong casino!

Stunned, I just sat there for a minute or two, trying to reconstruct exactly what had happened, trying to comprehend this double-fisted, thirty-second ambush. Was it possible that a major casino in Atlantic City would pull such a relatively penny-ante robbery? I could understand bringing in a "mechanic," but not blatantly mugging me, and right in front of my eyes!

There was an abrupt shift change, and a different dealer took over. My lady dealer avoided my eyes as she hastily exited the table. Still in shock, I looked at my watch and realized I had a bus to catch. Dejectedly, I cashed in my chips and then taxied over to the bus terminal. Once on board, I was able to think more clearly. I rewound that unbelievable thirty-second heist over and over again in my mind. I suddenly realized that I didn't *really* have to take the 3 o'clock bus—buses to New York ran every hour. What I *should* have done was *immediately* go over to the Casino Control Commission official in the casino, who would have promptly reviewed the videotape of the action at the table, and then justice would have been done. Or would it? Not according to the explanation—excuse?—I got later.

Now in New York, and thinking more lucidly, I waited until 9:00 the next morning, a Friday, and called the main office of the Casino Control Commission in Atlantic City. I would have called when I got home the night before, but I figured it was too late to dial them up.

The person who answered told me none of the Commissioners were in, and asked me to call back later. When I called back at 1:00, everybody was out to lunch. At four they were all gone for the day.

Undaunted, I called back Monday morning, and was immediately connected with a Mr. Cross (names have been changed to protect the guilty). I told the story of what had happened to me at the Gong casino on the previous Thursday, and his voice told me he was not enthusiastic about addressing my problem. He said the person who handled the Gong casino was unavailable, and to call again in two days. I called again two days later, only to be told that the man I needed to talk to was out of town, and to try again. I'll spare you details of the long and circuitous string of phone calls I made to the Commission (I later figured out that Mr. Cross was sloughing me off, hoping I would be discouraged and go away). He finally said Yes, he had at last spoken to the official in charge of monitoring the Gong casino and, surprise!, there were no cameras in operation at my table at the time of the heist.

Crushed, I hung up the phone and figured it was time to throw in the towel. There was no place else for me to go.

Years later, when I and thousand of others were taken in by a major casino's phony-baloney newspaper promotion, I again contacted the Casino Control Commission. This time I had the "smoking gun"—a complete and perfect paper trail of the scam! Did justice triumph this time? Was the casino nailed for its transgressions? More on that later.

The blatant Gong casino robbery rankled me for months—it still hurts today. After mulling it over and over I think I figured out why they pulled this cheap scam. Kirk Kerkorian can fly a casino executive all the way to Australia to tell Kerry Packer that the MGM Grand doesn't want his business, but what recourse does the casino have against a relatively penny-ante hit-and-run guy like myself? The answer is as simple as it is primitive. They mug him!

The Gambler Strikes Back, Part I

Did the casino make its point with me? You bet your ass it did. For months, every time I went to Atlantic City I avoided the Gong casino like the plague. I didn't go in for a drink or even to use their men's room. I don't think I would have gone there even if they'd had great King Crab claws.

Then, one day on the bus headed to Atlantic City, it suddenly dawned on me that I was doing it all *wrong*. Instead of avoiding the casino, I should use my wiles and hit back, but v-e-r-y carefully. They ripped me off for almost $2,000, so for the next twenty trips my primary goal would be to win $100 there each time. The Gong was about to taste the vengeance of my weapons of discipline and restraint—my "Hit and Run."

With trepidation—I was scared shitless—I returned to the Gong casino for the first time in eight months. With my $2,000 in seed money at an "outside" (non-pit) $10 minimum blackjack table—no baccarat pit tables for me!—I played blackjack as close to the chest as I ever played it in my life. Slowly, I ground away, painfully winning two $5 chips at a time. Every time I lost a hand it was a tug at my heart. After an eternity of betting, I finally ground out my $100 and headed directly for the cashier's cage. $100 down; a minimum of $1,900 more to go.

With winged feet I left the Gong casino. Even when I had won that $31,125 in Las Vegas so many years ago I don't think I experienced the same euphoria that I felt winning the crooked casino's $100.

Having broken the ice, my next visit to the casino was not so stressful. I even felt comfortable enough to return to the $25-minimum blackjack tables. I won $275 rather quickly. I hit and I ran.

I felt so invigorated and confident that I actually made a second foray to the Gong casino before boarding the bus home, and I won another $125.

Four hundred dollars from the Gong for the day! At that point I had recouped a two-trip total of $500 from the Gong's cashier's cage. Another grand-and-a-half to go. . . .

When I next returned to Atlantic City, I was no longer intimidated by the rogue casino. Not only was I at ease there, but I even made it my first stop off the bus so that, if I had time later, I'd go back for a second helping. I had time. And I had my second helping. Total win for the day at the Gong: $625.

Regrettably, the rest of that visit to the seashore was a total waste. The $625 I won from the Gong, and most of my $6,000 seed money were swept away by a string of losing tables all across the city. No one can win all the time, or even most of the time. However, no net loss could detract from the sweet satisfaction of winning that $625 at the hated Gong!

Through the years since then I've made a lot of hit-and-run trips to the seashore. There has been no pattern to my excursions, with one marked exception: I always make an obligatory pit stop at the hated Gong casino to win *something*. Perhaps it was bullheaded of me to once have spent an hour-and-a-half of my precious five-hour scheduled visit to Atlantic City just to grind out a meager $35 win there, but goddammit, that $35 was sweeter than the $600 I won at the next casino on my tour.

In recent years I've had to curtail my Atlantic City trips because of an unfortunate accident. I was run over, dragged, and seriously injured by a garbage truck. (My premature obituary even was printed in a local newspaper!) Though my visits are fewer than they were, one remnant of my former agenda remains rigidly in place: the obligatory visit to the Gong casino. And I still refuse to walk out the door without some of their money in my pocket!

I've always felt awkward telling people of being cheated by a major Atlantic City casino by having my chips stolen off the table right in front of my eyes. Many of my friends have looked at me skeptically when I told the story. Why would a multimillion-dollar casino risk its license to steal a couple of thousand in chips from a player?

My friends' understandably dubious reactions to my true story were somewhat answered by Abdul Jalib's article in the Summer 1998 issue of *The Intelligent Gambler*, where he wrote, "A further threat to the entire [gambling] industry is that the casinos commit crimes against skilled blackjack players . . . *[M]ajor Vegas casinos have literally stolen chips from skilled players.*"

So they rob the players in Las Vegas too!

If you examine casino practices closely, you'll see a pattern of lawlessness emerge. Blacklisted Mafiosi, though the law forbade their entrance to casinos, have been caught gambling—with hefty credit lines yet!—for which the casinos have been heavily fined. One time the kids standing in line at the Las Vegas Hilton, waiting to see the *Star Trek* show there, were allowed to play the slot machines! The greedy casino was fined a hefty $350,000 for that one.

The casinos can, have, and will cheat players, and they continue to get away with it because the Casino Control Commission looks the other way.

Jalib in his informative article recounts other criminal activity by the Las Vegas casinos. And adds that, "Eventually *60 Minutes* or some other show is going to give these crimes perpetuated by the casinos the publicity they deserve. . . ."

When they do, Buster, the shit will finally and deservedly hit the fan.

And if you still believe that the people running the casinos have either a modicum of decency or an ounce of compassion for the players, scholar Erika Gosker writes in the October 1999 in the *Elder Law Journal*:

> ...that some casinos send charter buses to nursing homes and senior centers right after beneficiaries receive their

Social Security checks. The industry has even coined terms such as "the third-of-the-month club" to describe these sought-after patrons.

Card Counting

I frequently hear blackjack players in Atlantic City bemoaning the fact that Casino Control Commission regulations have mandated that all the casinos are required to deal blackjack from an eight-deck shoe. If they had their druthers, these players would choose a single- or double-deck game, with hand-dealt cards.

An ugly incident in the 1970s involving Frank Sinatra in Atlantic City illustrates the point. He sat down at a blackjack table and demanded that the dealer use a single deck and deal manually. The pit boss explained that this couldn't be done, but Sinatra made a scene and the pit boss caved in and permitted the dealer to hand-deal with a single deck. The shit really hit the fan, as the dealer, the pit boss, the casino—and Sinatra—were all taken to task for the transgression, and the casino was heavily fined.

Me, I'm delighted with the game the way it is dealt from the shoe. Sure, the odds are slightly more in the casino's favor with multiple deck action, but the peace of mind I have at the table, knowing I'm getting an honest deal for my buck, is well worth it. I no longer wager my money on non-shoe-dealt games.

When I started my casino prowling years ago in Las Vegas, there were no shoes for blackjack. The only shoes in use were at the baccarat table. All blackjack games were single- or double-deck affairs. There were times when I played all the hands at a table and, dammit, whatever I had, the dealer had better. I vividly recall once having a nice line-up of all 20s—and the dealer wiped me out with his 21.

Don't misunderstand me. I'm not saying that I was cheated, but

I am saying that with what I've learned since, I can fairly say that I very well *could* have been cheated.

Let me tell you what happened. I am in the book trade, and so as a yearly ritual, when the booksellers' annual convention comes around I make it my business to attend. One year, one of the major publishers featured a biography of Nick the Greek, one of the legendary gamblers of the mid-Twentieth Century. As a gimmick at the publisher's booth, they had a magician doing card tricks and demonstrating how he could manipulate the cards in blackjack. He shuffled the cards and had someone cut them. Then, to my amazement, he told the audience that he would deal four hands of 20s and deal himself a blackjack, and specifically with a red King and a black Jack. He then proceeded to do it!

Being suspicious by nature, I figured his deck was gimmicked, so I went over to a cigar store in the hotel and bought a deck of cards, which I took over to the performer.

"Here, let's see you do it again with *my* cards."

He took off the cellophane and removed the Jokers. He shuffled the cards thoroughly and I personally cut the deck. "Like before," he announced. "I'll deal four hands of 20s, and a red King and a black Jack."

And damned if he didn't do it again—with my cards! Needless to say, that cured me forever of playing blackjack with a dealer who is tossing out the cards manually. It should also give you food for thought.

For no rational reason, I do not like to enter a blackjack game when a shoe is near its end. My preference dovetails with many of the Atlantic City casinos, who don't permit mid-shoe entry at the $25-and-up tables. This restriction, intended to thwart card-counters, strikes me as paranoid because most all Atlantic City blackjack games are played with 8-deck shoes, with the dealer cutting the shoe at least two decks back. No more than six decks are dealt before the yellow shuffle card appears. With a hundred or more cards of the 416 cards "buried" in the shoe, how anyone can hope to successfully "count" the cards is beyond me.

♠ ♠ ♠ ♠ ♠

And as for "card counters" who write self-celebrating articles and books on how they can cream the casinos, I have my doubts. I won't say that you shouldn't read the articles and books by these so-called experts, but just take them with a good pinch of salt. I'm not the only one around who has his doubts. Frank Scoblete, a noted writer on casino gambling, wrote in the September 1998 issue of the *Atlantic City* magazine, "The best blackjack 'counter' that I ever played with made no more than $30,000 in a good year—and he played every day! . . . Unless [he] is a part of a huge team that bets in the tens of thousands of dollars, the prospects of making millions are about the same as being hit with lightning." Scoblete adds, "[I]f I owned a casino, I'd have a big sign outside, 'Card Counters Welcome!'"

Funny, that same sentiment was voiced by a Las Vegas casino executive when I asked about Thorp, who wrote *Beat the Dealer*. The executive laughed heartily and told me, "If Thorp calls me next time he's in Vegas, I'll send a limo to pick him up at the airport."

With an eight-deck shoe, and the dealer cutting at least two decks in, how in hell can *anyone* successfully count the cards?

Even with the eight decks stacked in their favor, paranoia apparently has taken hold of the Atlantic City casino front offices again. Phil Roura, in his regular Sunday column in the New York *Daily News*, reports that the Casino Control Commission made a rather curious new ruling in regard to card counters. Now get this, boys and girls: "If a [suspected] card counter is spotted at a blackjack table, the casino will now be allowed to lower the maximum bet there to $50. Pit bosses, however, may inform the other players at the table that the new minimum *doesn't* apply to them."

Roura closed the column with a sarcastically quizzical, "Huh?"

Remember: whenever casinos can cook up new ways to screw their customers, they promptly implement them, frequently in cahoots with an often pliant Casino Control Commission.

Illegal Casinos

With the proliferation of Native American and State-sanctioned casinos all across America, and with lottery games available everywhere, it is easy to forget that illegal wagering, and even clandestine casinos, are still alive and doing well across America.

There are two good reasons street-corner bookies and illegal numbers banks still thrive. Lotto sellers and Off-Track Betting parlors notwithstanding, you get better odds outside the law and, if you win, there is no tax to pay.

Illegal casinos operated openly all during the 1920s and on through the 1950s. Colonel Bradley's Palm Beach Club in Florida was a national open secret for decades. It was a classy joint where well-heeled patrons included top theater people, all of whom got an honest shake.

Illegal casinos operated openly in Saratoga Springs, New York, but only during the racing season. Even Atlantic City had a thriving illegal casino before the legal ones arrived. The famous 500 Club, where Jerry Lewis first teamed up with Dean Martin, had a lively gaming operation in its back room. Ben Marden's Riviera in New Jersey, just across the bridge from Manhattan, boasted a full casino. In New York State, both Montauk and Catskill resort hotels had casino gambling. Lexington, Kentucky and Gary, Indiana were also notorious casino towns. How many people know that a young Dean Martin got his start as a blackjack dealer in Gary?

Even today there are illegal casinos in operation in New York City. A fancy townhouse on East 36th Street was busted only a couple of years ago. As I write this, I hear there's a full casino going strong in Greenwich Village. Chinatown is reported to have a dozen or more, but they offer a menu of strange table games and cater strictly to a Chinese clientele.

Through the years I've had my share of experiences in illegal casinos. As a kid, when I'd go up to the Catskills with my family, I'd gaze in wonder at the magical machines with their colorful whirling wheels offering cherries, lemons, and bells, and that would from time-to-time pour out torrents of coins to the lucky player. What a thrill it was when I hit the jackpot for the first time, and was showered with what seemed then to be all the nickels in the world! I don't think even my thrill when I hit the Hacienda quarter progressive machine one Christmas day in Las Vegas for $5,000 could match that childhood memory.

In 1946, in Los Angeles for the first time, I couldn't resist the lure of going onto the *Rex*, a mob-owned gambling ship operating three miles offshore from Santa Monica. It was the first time I had ever seen a full casino in operation. (Outside of the slot machines, the Catskills only had roulette wheels in action, and that, was only in the evenings.)

On the *Rex* I timidly tried my luck at the blackjack table but, feeling uncomfortable with the new game, I quickly retreated to the banks of slot machines, with less luck than my Catskill initiation of years before. Aside from its full casino, my main memory of the *Rex* is what appeared to be one whole deck of toilets. The mob was forced to install them in order to comply with some harebrained maritime law regulation that was passed at that time solely as a harassment ploy for gambling ships.

My next experience with clandestine casinos was in the 1970s. My then-girl friend had had a recent operation and decided that, with a little financial help from me, the hot baths in Hot Springs, Arkansas would be conducive to her recovery. On a whim, I decided to fly down with her and see what Hot Springs was all about.

To my surprise and delight, the city was dotted with illegal full casinos, slot machines and all. Playing cautiously, I managed to eke out my expenses, plus a few bucks extra for a couple of gourmet meals with my lady friend before flying back to New York.

Looking back at my forays in illegal casinos, I guess I was lucky that I got away cheap. How honest a clandestine casino may be is a moot question. There are problems and obstacles that an illegal casino has to contend with that an above-board casino does not, the main one being "the pad." In gambling vernacular, the pad is the payoff, the hefty graft that has to be funneled to public officials so they'll look the other way. You better believe the cash involved—and it's all cash—is no inconsequential sum. Depending on the size of the operation, the payoffs can extend from local cops on the beat all the way up to the Governor's mansion. In the 1920s, New York's Mayor Jimmy Walker had to leave office under a cloud of gambling-related scandal. In the 1940s another New York Mayor, Bill O'Dwyer, hastily resigned when investigators followed a paper trail of illegal gambling payoffs all the way up to City Hall.

When the cash-off-the-top has to go for protection, mob-operated casinos have to resort to "special measures" to insure profits, that is, to cheat. Gimmicked roulette tables, loaded dice that are switched in and out of the game, and "mechanics" (card sharks) that deal blackjack, are some of their instruments. With honest casinos (an oxymoron?), house percentages are already putting two strikes on the player; a gaffed casino's crooked game just about guarantees the sucker in an illegal casino a sure-thing strike-out.

Should you patronize illegal gambling operations? When it comes to casinos, the answer is a resounding NO! As for those of you out there who insist on betting on the nags, as well as you retards who throw away your money on numbers, I have to give a qualified Yes. Street-corner bookies will give you a better bang for your buck, as their odds are shorter than the odds of the track and OTBs. As for the numbers, the state will give you a flat-out rip-off 500-to-1 payoff, while your friendly local numbers bank will give you 600-to-1, also a shameless rip-off, but at least a better one than the state's.

Better yet stay away from nags and numbers. If you must gamble, hit and run at your nearest casino. You might even come home with some of their cash in your pocket, an unlikely scenario if you play Lotto, numbers, and nags.

And playing in illegal casinos has its hazards. This was vividly illustrated when the New York *Daily News* reported on October 5, 1998 that three gunmen burst into an around-the-clock illegal gambling club in Brooklyn, shot one of the dealers, and robbed the players of all their cash and jewelry.

One of the gunmen was captured but the other two were able to escape with the loot.

Anatomy of a Casino Promotion, or How I Got Bamboozled

As I've said, I never—but NEVER—put MY money into slot machines. Sure, I'll play the slots, but I always make it a rule to first win the money at the tables, and then pump it into the machines.

One Sunday, in the Spring of 1997, I was a fool. But only one of hundreds of fools. We'd all flocked to an Atlantic City casino, lured there by an irresistible *same-day-50%-rebate-at-the-slot-machines* offer, laid out in a razzle-dazzle quarter-page display ad in the previous Friday's New York newspaper. Sadly, it turned out to be nothing more than the classic bait-and-switch.

I saved everything, so that I have a complete paper trail, laying out the anatomy of the rip-off. The casino has no defense.

You would think that justice would eventually triumph. So did I. All the ads, the direct-mail the casino sent me, the material I was given there, along with the letters I wrote, including copies of all my evidence, plus the replies I got back in reference to the apparent scam, including one from the Governor of New Jersey—let them all speak for themselves. I saved them all.

It's all laid out. You be the judge.

Even though it was a very transparent and clumsy scam—so clumsy that the casino didn't even bother to cover its ass and arrogantly repeated the rip-off ad verbatim on the following Friday!

I was infuriated. I set out to "get" them.

I wrote to the Chairman of the Casino Control Commission and I also wrote to the whole Casino Control Commission, to every damn member, all by Registered Mail, Return Receipt Requested. I wrote to the Governor. I wrote to the New Jersey Attorney General. I wrote to the United States Postal Inspectors, as the United States mail was used in the scam. I wrote to the Consumer Advocate of New York City. (New York newspapers were utilized for the rip-off.) I wrote to the New York State Attorney General. I wrote to—hell, why go on? You get the gist.

It is now more than four years since I sent all my letters with Xeroxes of all my hard evidence to everybody with clout who could possibly rectify the injustice, not only for me, but also for the other hundreds—maybe even thousands—of casino patrons who were victimized.

Was justice done? Let's look at the record.

Diane M. Legreide, a Vice Chairman of the Casino Control Commission, wrote me that "the Chairman has forwarded your materials to the New Jersey Division of Gaming Enforcement for investigation. Please be assured that the situation will be looked into *and we will keep you abreast of the matter.* [Italics mine.]

One Commissioner, Leanna Brown, also replied. "I know it is not easy to duplicate and send many copies [out] at $2.39 each for postage. However, it is appreciated. Too few people make this effort. I have been concerned by some of the marketing techniques used by the casinos, especially this year. As you know [No, I didn't know. It wasn't publicized, to be sure.—A.B.L.], we no longer regulate marketing, but incidents like this illustrate why we did once.

"I will be waiting as will you with much interest for the D.G.E. [Department of Gaming Enforcement] response."

Yes, I am too, Commissioner Brown, but to date, I'm still waiting. . . .

The other Commissioner, James R. Hurley, who also received my registered letter along with my dossier never even bothered to respond.

Now let's see what has happened since I lodged my complaints in May, 1997, to both State and Federal regulatory agencies in regard to the casino's repeated ads that lured me, and thousands of others like me, to their casino with an offer they had no intention of honoring.

The Chairman of the Casino Control Commission sent my Registered Letter and my "smoking gun" evidence to the New Jersey Division of Gaming Enforcement "for investigation and appropriate action," and thanked me for "taking the time to bring this matter to my attention."

Governor Whitman forwarded my letter and the "smoking gun" evidence to the Treasurer of New Jersey "to review my concerns," and noted "that a response will be sent to you directly on my behalf."

Deputy Attorney General of New Jersey Timothy C. Ficci responded that "the Division is investigating the matter, *and, subsequent to your letter, has received other complaints regarding this promotion.*"

To date I have calculated that it took less time to investigate Watergate than it has taken these people to nail the casino. As of July, 2000, I have yet to hear from the Chairman of the Casino Control Commission, the two Vice-Chairmen of the Casino Control Commission, the Treasurer of the State of New Jersey, or its Attorney General, who had an investigation under way on July

15,1997, or in fact from *any* of the many officials in New Jersey to whom I sent my solid evidence.

With no response and no action by any of the agencies that are allegedly there to protect my interests, I could only bitterly write it off as a Lost Cause, I thought. I had tried the legal route to obtain justice for myself and the others that were taken in, but being a novice at suing, I learned that I came to my attorney too late in the game. Famed Philadelphia lawyer (and dear friend) Albert B. Gerber regretfully told me that I should have seen him before I (finally) got my refund. Then he could have started the wheels in motion for a Class Action suit against the casino.

Frankly I'm at a loss why blatant violations by the casinos are often ignored by regulatory agencies that profess to exist to protect the public. It appears that the casinos and the owners are Sacred Cows that are above the law.

One day I picked up a copy of a New York tabloid, and suddenly there it was! Now all the pieces fit together. The Casino Control Commission released the figures for that quarter of the year, and they were spectacular. The casinos were raking in megabuck operating profits. They all made big gains.

All but one. The scam casino was at the bottom of the list—with an utterly disastrous *loss* for the period!

Perhaps I'm reading more into it than is there, but I would think that a casino, sinking steadily for the quarter, as the bait-and-switch casino was, would be tempted to resort to desperate measures to stem the decline. I can easily imagine how much *more* of a fiasco the quarter would have been for it had they not fattened their bottom line by taking money from me, and thousands more like me, with their too-good-to-be-true promotion that *was* too good to be true.

Lotto

✓ The Great Rip-off
✓ Powerball-oney
✓ One Man's Trash is Another Man's Cash

The Great Rip-off

QUICK RIDDLE: What has six balls and screws you
              three-times-a-week?
ANSWER: Lotto.

If you go out and buy yourself a lottery ticket today, the odds
are literally millions-to-one against you hitting the jackpot. However,
if you placed a bet that the company running your state lottery is
shadowy, your odds would be a lot better. California, New York,
and New Jersey, among other states, had the fog of scandal hanging over their lottery operations, and there was even a Federal Grand
Jury in Texas probing the activities of one lottery company.

Lottery operators are a cunning lot. Not content with profits
from the New York daily numbers drawings and the dozen or more
scratch-off "games" for sale everywhere, the lottery crowd in Albany
schemed up a neat way to circumvent New York's long-standing
legal prohibition against casino gambling games. Keno, a casino
mainstay in both New Jersey and Nevada casinos, was finessed into
New York State under the alias of Quick-Draw.

Quick-Draw is a video numbers game that is flashed on television screens in many New York bars and delis. A new game runs
every five minutes.

Keno and Quick-Draw are identical in concept, except that
Quick-Draw has fewer numbers and smaller payoffs and, as bad a

bet as Keno is, Quick-Draw is even worse.

How the lottery wheeler-dealers got it through the New York State Legislature is one for the books. To begin with, the lottery company honcho running all the New York State Lottery games was a high school pal of New York State Governor George Pataki and one of Pataki's earliest financial backers. A fortuitous coincidence?

To offer the casino game to the state legislature in a bill by itself would have surely killed it, so Governor Pataki finessed the Keno-type game through the legislature by piggybacking it onto a popular tax-cut bill during an election year. And that's how New York got its casino lottery game into every-other gin mill and corner deli in the state.

Without even taking into account any back-room hanky-panky, ask yourself are YOU ahead for all the lottery tickets you've bought? Of course the answer is NO. Do you actually personally know any people who are ahead of the game? The probable answer again is NO, *Nada, Nyet.*

Indeed, the lottery drawing you see on TV isn't guaranteed to be honest. Pennsylvania was rocked by lottery scandal a few years back when the ping-pong balls in the glass blowers were found to be rigged; only balls bearing pre-chosen numbers were light enough to rise to the top. The other numbered ping-pong balls were weighted so they couldn't make it up the tube.

The lottery people sure aren't rooting for you to win. In case you don't believe me, check this out. A few years back California had a scratch-off promotion where a few "lucky" players would win a chance to spin a carnival-type wheel on TV, with cash prizes spread out all over the wheel, ranging from a few thousand dollars to one sliver-of-a-niche labeled one million dollars. A portly lady who scratched off a chance to win gave the wheel a hefty spin. To her delight, it stopped on the million-dollar space! No dispute over that.

Reruns of the television tape *plainly* show that it landed on the million-dollar mark. Overjoyed, the obese lady jumped up and down with joy over her good fortune. Her jumping created enough of a tremor to jar the wheel and nudge it over into a many-fewer-thousands-of-dollars slot, which the oily emcee quickly announced as the amount she was going to receive.

It took our heavy heroine more than a year in the California courts—at great expense to the lady—finally to force the lottery people to give her the million dollars that she'd rightfully won.

Lottery shenanigans aren't limited to the continental United States, Alaska, and Hawaii. Italy is still reverberating from a monstrous fiasco that almost precipitated a regional insurrection. Somehow, the machines numbering the Italian lottery tickets momentarily stalled at one number—the jackpot number. As fate would have it, that batch of tickets all ended up in one small Italian town. When the *paisans* checked their tickets against the winning numbers, they all went wild with joy. Celebrating their apparent windfall with gusto, they began spending wildly, really living it up.

When the mob of lucky ticket holders went off to Rome to collect their millions of lira in winnings, the horrified lottery operators had to split the jackpot prize into proportionate shares, which gave each of the winners about enough money to buy a couple of pizzas. I won't go into the gory details of the outcome, except to note that it was very violent, and that the lottery people quickly found themselves a new printer.

Of all the lottery "games," the worst bet of all is the instant scratch-off. When these games were first introduced in New York years ago, I, like so many other New Yorkers, tried my luck. From time-to-time I'd invest a couple of dollars, usually without much success.

Sure, I'd get a $2 or $5 winner occasionally, but most of the time I found that I had just pissed away a coupla bucks. Yet somewhere in my psyche, as most lottery players fantasize, I expected that my Pot of Gold was waiting for me, maybe with the next ticket I bought.

New York skyscrapers have more in-and-out lobby activity than some airports, which allows lobby cigar stand operators to make a living. On my way up to see a publisher, I impulsively stopped at a lobby stand and bought a $1 lottery ticket. I scratched it off in the elevator and was delighted to find I had a $25 winner. On my way out I happily cashed my winning ticket. What the proprietor said as he counted out the $25 cured me *forever* from buying anymore scratch-off lottery tickets.

"Jeez, yer one lucky guy. In a year an' a haff I mustda sold a coupla hunnerd thou' tickets, and yer da' foist $25 winner I ever seen."

There are flukes, of course, as lightning must strike somewhere. Once, Lyle Stuart took some employees and kin out for lunch. Impulsively, he stopped off and bought a $1 lottery for each of his guests, putting a ticket at each place setting. His daughter Sandy learned two nights later that she had a $5,000 winner.

To sum it all up, my advice to you is to avoid the state lotteries in all their razzle-dazzle shapes and forms. They're all rip-offs. You can't win, you won't win; don't waste your money. If you think playing your "lucky numbers" will be the key to a life of wealth and ease, think again. Most of the pitifully few winners of New York State Weekly Lotto jackpots have won by the dumb-luck "Quick-Pick" ticket, where the Lotto computer selects your numbers.

The New York *Daily News* reported that there were five winners of the $40 million jackpot of February 26, 1998. The headline of this story: "A Quick-Pick Trip to Wealth."

All five of the winners did it with Quick-Pick tickets!

Outside of the Quick-Pick method, the only way I can suggest for you to pick a winner is to buy a monkey. A man in California had his pet monkey pick out numbered ping-pong balls from a cardboard box. You guessed it, pal. The monkey unerringly picked out the wining lottery numbers, guaranteeing his owner a life of ease and for himself a lifetime supply of bananas.

If you don't happen to own a pet monkey, then the next wisest thing is just not to buy any rip-off state lottery tickets.

Early on, the lottery gang realized that lottery players are nothing but a flock of sheep, easy marks to be fleeced again and again. Bad enough that a pitifully small amount of lottery profits are allocated for prizes, but when some schmuck holding a winning ticket doesn't redeem it—the ticket expires a year from purchase—the state claims that it "recycles" the unclaimed prize "into the prize pool," which is total bullshit.

A $13.3-million-dollar winning Lotto ticket was purchased on June 3, 1996 and expired on the following June 3, 1997. Did the Lottery boys in Albany start off the next week's Lotto jackpot with the unclaimed $13.3 million, or with any of the $46.6 million in unclaimed prize money from Take Five, Pick 10, Quick-Draw, and all the multifarious scratch-off games? You bet your sweet ass they didn't!

Would you believe that, as the New York *Daily News* reported, a mind-boggling $59,900,000 in Lottery prize winnings went unclaimed *in the year 1997 alone?*

Lottery players in general are proven losers, but especially those who blunder into buying a winning ticket and then don't even bother to check the numbers to see if they won!

It has been said that some people really don't want to win. When I see that almost $60 million was incredibly ceded back to the Lottery cabal by these born losers, I tend to agree.

The Spaniard who had a winning Lottery ticket for a January 1998 drawing can be forgiven for not cashing it. The unfortunate fellow died prior to the drawing and was buried along with the winning ticket in his pocket. The Associated Press news story didn't say whether or not his grieving relatives later dug up the corpse to retrieve the ticket.

Like your local Chinese laundry man says: no tickee, no washee. Same goes for New York State. The Associated Press reported on August 8, 1998 that Governor Pataki vetoed a bill that would have merely given a Long Island cab driver a *hearing* on his claim that he mistakenly tossed away a $7.4 million ticket.

The hearing would have given him the *chance* to become the first Lotto winner in the state to be awarded a prize without a ticket. Incredibly, Pataki reported that on that particular drawing there were 28,056 unclaimed prizes! According to the Governor, this could have resulted in *thousands* of hearings for that one drawing alone. All of the 28,056 unclaimed winning tickets for that drawing became invalid, worthless.

BLOWING A WINDFALL was a headline in the November 28, 1998 New York *Daily News*, noting that "[the] Lotto winner is yet to claim [his] $2,500,000 prize" before the deadline.

By New York State law, all unclaimed lottery prize money is put directly into the General Fund, which can then be used for *any* purpose the State cares to use it for.

Only nine days after lottery officials' recycling assurance, the following startling headline was splashed across the front page of the Sunday New York *Post* of November 30, 1998:

LOTTO PRIZES SHRINK

So much for New York State's Lotto's bogus assertion that they are plowing back all the tens of million dollars of lottery prize money that the unfortunate suckers neglect to collect.

Consider one Brooklyn family's sad plight. THE SEARCH IS ON FOR A $5M TICKET was the New York *Daily News* headline on Friday the Thirteenth of March, 1998. If the ticket isn't cashed in by April 9, 1998, the story went on, then like the other tens of millions in unclaimed prizes, the $5 million will go back to the state. Maybe Friday the Thirteenth was an omen for the Griffins of Brooklyn, who always buy their Lotto tickets from JGJ Liquors and always play the same numbers, which happened to be the winning numbers on the missing $5 million ticket.

They ransacked their apartment over and over again looking for the ticket they knew they bought, but no luck. Even though I believed them, the *Daily News* believed them, and probably even the lottery officials believed them, regretfully the officials gave their version of "No tickee, No washee": If you don't present the ticket you don't collect, period.

To repeat, if you're silly enough to waste your money on a lottery ticket, at least have enough brain matter to hang on to it and check it for a winner.

As dumb as lottery players are, in my estimation horse players are even dumber. Years ago I came to the realization that horses are smarter than people. After all, I've never heard of a horse that bet on a man. Have you?

The racetracks take an unconscionable percentage of dough out of the betting pool, but compared to OTB, they're benevolent. Off-Track Betting slices the pie even thinner.

And, like the lottery fools who don't bother to cash their winning tickets, some pony players piss away their winnings also by not cashing in. Since 1990, a staggering $70 million in horse bets has gone unclaimed. On September 13, 1998, the New York *Post* noted that $8 million had gone unclaimed in 1998 alone. The money just galloped out of the bettors' pockets and into the New York State treasury.

The stupidity of OTB players is exemplified by the player who bets there, then doesn't wait around to watch the race. When he opens his newspaper the next day and doesn't see his horse in the money, he throws away his ticket. What he forgets is the possibility that his nag was scratched, and didn't run at all. In that case, he is entitled to a full refund.

Powerball-oney

As piss-poor a bet as Lotto is, Powerball—played in twenty states and the District of Columbia—makes Lotto look good. Both are rip-offs, stealing money from the people who can least afford to lose it. With Lotto you have at least a wisp of a fighting chance with "only" 13 million-to-1 odds against you.

Powerball can well afford to dangle a $195-million jackpot in front of foolish players (the jackpot in one instance). Why not? The citizens have enriched the Powerball operators by buying more than a billion dollars in losing tickets prior to the drawing!

What makes Powerball a classic con game is the way it's set up. First, the player has to pick the correct five numbers from a pool of forty-nine numbers. Even if he nails the five, he still does-n't win the jackpot.

To win the multi-million-dollar jackpot he also has to pick the Powerball number—a *sixth* number from a *separate* set of forty-two numbers—which brings the odds of winning up to an astronomi-cal 80,100,000-to-1.

The evil genius who thought up this game is a prime candi-date for being roasted in the eternal fires of Hell alongside of Hitler, Stalin, Idi Amin, and the Boston Strangler. The Pearly Gates of Heaven are forever closed to the inventor of Powerball.

The mind-boggling multi-million dollar jackpots ignited Powerball fever in the Northeastern states. Tiny Rhode Island once sold more than a million tickets for a single drawing—one ticket for every man, woman, and child in the state! Washington, D.C. even outdid Rhode Island; there they sold 1,700,000 tickets for a single drawing—*two* tickets for every resident of the District of Columbia!

New York and New Jersey players really went wild. With Connecticut being the closest Powerball state, they stampeded across the border. Traffic jams headed north were crippling, with all roads tied up for hours, day and night. The tiny hamlet of Byrum, Connecticut, which happens to be the closest town to the New York State line, got hit like a ton of bricks. Powerball just about paralyzed the little town. The local barber was forced to close shop early because his regular customers couldn't park anywhere within ten blocks of his shop.

One store owner in New Castle, Delaware, chose to close rather than deal with the endless line that stretched out the door of his little shop. He had to call the police to handle the mob of customers who were furious at having to leave empty-handed after waiting four hours to put down their bets.

When the drawing finally took place on Wednesday, May 20, 1998, there was just one 195 million dollar winner, a ticket sold at the Lakeside Country Store in Walworth County, Wisconsin. Interestingly, the previous Powerball record jackpot was $111.2 million, it was also sold in Wisconsin.

The ballyhooed $195-million jackpot figure is a deception. The $195 million is paid out to the tune of about $8 million a year for twenty-five years. The slick operators deposit just enough money in a bank to throw off $8 million yearly in interest. At the end of twenty-five years they withdraw the whole amount, so the $195-million jackpot didn't cost them a penny!

If the winner opts for a cash payment—which the winner did—the loudly touted $195 million suddenly shrinks to $104 million. After taxes, the winner netted $68 million. Not an inconsequential sum, to be sure, but a long distance from the heralded $195 million.

As for the tens of thousands from New York and New Jersey who stampeded into Connecticut and waited on long lines for hours on end, eager to pump their many millions of dollars into the Powerball machines, all they got for their money was the shaft.

Will this discourage them? Not likely.

One Man's Trash Is Another Man's Cash

My no-cost Lotto windfalls were all thanks to my sharp eye. I've always made it a point to pick up any lottery tickets (without heel marks) that I spot on the sidewalks of Manhattan. You'd be amazed by how many "live" tickets I've found through the years-they number in the dozens. Sadly, most of the "live" tickets I've found have been as good as dead-losers. Once I found a batch of ten tickets, neatly tacked together with a paper clip. Not a winner in the lot! Through the years, seven of the winning tickets I've found have been the instant kind, the scratch-offs. The games were so complicated and instructions so unclear that the buyers had discarded the winning tickets, not realizing they had won.

I found my big winner, the $1300 ticket, on Fifth Avenue in front of the New York Public Library. It was Sunday and my wife was displaying her artwork near the corner of 40th Street. Needing a pick-me-up, she asked me to please go get her a Coke from the hot dog vendor on 42nd Street. Halfway down the block I spied a lone Lotto ticket and picked it up. It was for Lotto Forty, a game that has since been discontinued in New York, and it was to be run the next day. The next morning, sitting in the back of a bus, I suddenly remembered that I had that Lotto Forty ticket in my pocket. I opened my copy of the Daily News. Incredulously, I looked at the numbers and I looked at the ticket. Whoever had bought it had correctly picked five out of six of the winning numbers! The purchaser had only missed the sixth--the jackpot number--by one digit (the sixth number picked was 23, it should have been 24).

The next day I went to the lottery headquarters in the World Trade Center and picked up a check from them for $1300. While I was there, a most happy feller with a smile from ear to ear bounced in with a winning ticket worth $5000 from New York's daily numbers game. His smile disappeared when they ran his name through the computer and found that he was a tax delinquent to the tune of $3600, which they promptly deducted from his winnings. Having witnessed this, I was able to alert one of the warehouse packers who had hit for a nice few thousand. He prudently sent his cousin to collect the winnings.

Luck

Monkey Dice

"I don't believe in 'luck.' For all that I care, a monkey could roll the dice!" I guess I repeated this mantra so often that publisher Lyle Stuart quoted it in one of his gambling books.

One day I got a call from Lyle asking me to meet him in front of my Manhattan office. He said it was important, and that he was coming over from New Jersey to give me "something."

Mystified, I waited outside.

Lyle drove up and rolled down the window of his Mercedes, handing me a large oblong package. Smiling mischievously, he announced, "Okay, kid—here's something you've always wanted," and drove away.

I now own a wind-up mechanical monkey that gives a little chatter, does a little dance, and tosses out a small pair of dice from a cup in his right paw.

I Don't Believe in Luck

But . . . As I have said so many times, I don't believe in luck. People make their own luck. My philosophy is, and has always been, that I wouldn't care if a zebra dealt the cards, or if a monkey rolled the dice. I tell you this as a preamble to two memorable episodes I witnessed during two blackjack sessions at Atlantic City casinos.

The first was at the Showboat, where I was sitting a couple of spots away from a loud-mouthed kid, whom I immediately pegged as a novice. Yet the way the cards were coming his way, he didn't have to know much. From the very first deal he was off-and-running.

He just couldn't lose. He turned up blackjack-after-blackjack, and when he missed a blackjack he got 20s and 21s. He wasn't betting big; the dumb kid wouldn't budge over the one-green-chip minimum, even though he won hand-after-hand-after-hand.

Even playing it so close to the vest, he still had a fairly decent pile of chips in front of him by the end of the shoe. He showed a very cavalier, take-it-for-granted attitude about what had happened as he leisurely picked up his chips and wandered over to a craps table. I never saw the kid again, but I'm pretty sure no matter how many more blackjack tables he gambles at for the rest of his life, this singular episode will stand out as his One Shoe of Fame. I only hope the kid appreciated it. I did.

The second episode happened in the $25-minimum blackjack pit at the Atlantic City Sands. Taking the two contiguous seats at "first base"—I play two hands—I found myself next to a flashily dressed Italian lady who must have applied Chanel No. 5 with a garden hose. To nail down my spot prior to the dealing of the shoe, I put a green chip on each of the two open spaces. I could see Miss Naples was visibly annoyed—she obviously wanted my other spot—but with a typical Latin shrug of the shoulders she settled down with her single spot. In retrospect I would have been overjoyed to have given her that second spot. Financially, I would have been far better off. On the other hand, Miss Naples, limited to her solitary spot, began her spectacular run, something she or I will never forget. Never, but *never*, have I seen so many blackjacks in the run of a shoe. After her fourth blackjack in a row even she became a little uneasy with the unreality of it all.

If I myself hadn't happened to cut the cards on that particular shoe I would have sworn that the fix was in. It was truly one shoe for the books! And the lady was a High Roller. The table had a $2,500 limit, and she often bet the limit. It was mind-boggling to see her rake in all those purple and yellow chips as the piles of chips before her just grew higher and higher.

When the shoe was finished, the pit bosses came around to survey the damage. The figure bandied about was $62,000—all from that one shoe. During the entire run of the shoe I recall her only losing maybe four or five hands, a stunning streak. (No, it never happened to me. I never even came close.) Was I jealous? You're damn right I was. Why, oh why, couldn't it have happened to me? Some day my turn will come. . . .

Can it happen to you? Sure, it can. I only recount these two episodes to show you that it can happen to someone.

Lucky Casinos

As a rule, people who think there are "lucky" casinos also believe in lucky numbers, lucky days, lucky charms, and astrology. As for myself, after four decades of casino-hopping I don't believe there is any such thing as a "lucky" casino. I will say that there are two casinos—one in Las Vegas and one in Atlantic City, where I have won consistently: the Sahara in Las Vegas, and Trump Plaza in Atlantic City.

In retrospect, had I just gambled at only these two casinos and then gone directly home, I would be a much richer man today. Too often I took their money and promptly lost it at the next casino.

The Sahara was a money-making machine for me almost from the start. I won there regularly. Oh, I may have walked out and dropped it at the casino next door, but at the Sahara I almost *expected* to win. Maybe my positive mental attitude helped, for I could do no wrong at the Sahara tables.

One particular visit was a pivotal point with the Sahara and me. I had flown to Las Vegas for a weekend. As usual on Sunday night, I worked my way up the Strip to the casino closest to the airport, careful not to cut it too close to departure time.

Safely checked in at McCarran Airport, my hand luggage dumped in a seventy-five-cent rental locker close at hand, I let myself go, and headed directly to the bar for a couple of stiff vodkas-and-grapefruit juice.

Why not? I had $3,600 in winnings, and I was only a few yards away from the boarding gate. But, as Shakespeare so aptly phrased it, "There's many a slip twixt the cup and the lip." The slip here was the dreaded announcement over the PA system that my TWA flight was delayed—for four goddam hours! Now well-oiled, I left the airport bar and returned to the Strip—where I taxied straight to the Sahara.

Once there, I won immediately and consistently. It was a snap. With forty-five minutes to go before the new departure time, I picked up my winning chips, another $5,000, and headed directly to the cashier's cage. Counting out all that fresh new Sahara folding money there, I just couldn't resist a parting shot.

"See you next trip," which translated into "Fuck you, Sahara, I'm going straight home with your money."

Suddenly, I felt a huge beefy arm around my shoulders. It was Frank Portnoy, a casino executive whom I had known casually through the years. In general I tend to keep my distance from dealers, pit bosses, and casino executives.

"Arnold," he began, all the while eyeing me as I stuffed the large roll of bills into my inside breast pocket, "Why don't you stay over? In fact, *any time* you come to Vegas I want you to be our guest." He paused for a moment, then added in a lower key, almost in a hoarse whisper, "Give us a chance to win it back." I had won so consistently at the Sahara—not a helluva lot at any one time, but a little almost every time.

Three months later, to my surprise, I got a phone call from Frank.

"Arnold, I'm in New York—for the first time in twenty-five years."

I didn't make the connection with my plundering of the Sahara's bankroll until he invited himself over to my book company loft and invited me out for lunch. It was obvious from the way his conversation—or should I say interrogation—went that he had been sent East by the Sahara to see who the hell I was and what the hell I did.

As the Sahara had treated me so well, I did the classy thing: I called my ticket broker and treated Frank to two Broadway shows while he was in New York.

Luck Reconsidered

My firm conviction that there is no such thing as "luck" occasionally wavers when I read stories like that of Steve and Peggy Hailes of Michigan, who motored to Onida, Wisconsin to celebrate a relative's birthday. On their way to the birthday party they stopped off at Onida One-Stop for gas. While waiting for service, Peggy wandered over to the slot machines in the back. "I just put a few quarters in that I had in my pocketbook and then it happened."

"It" was a $1,252,594.92 jackpot.

"It" can happen at Keno, too. When I see hoards of people

laboriously marking up Keno tickets with their "lucky" numbers, I have to remember Shirley Corbin of Altamont, Illinois, who hit for $10,968.40 at Sam's Town Casino in Las Vegas. What was "Lucky" Shirley's secret numbers-picking method? She simply marked off the whole top row, the first ten numbers on the ticket, and *voila*! Eight of her ten numbers were called for the eleven-grand payout.

Friday the 13th means diddly to me, but for some timid souls it's a harbinger of bad luck. One hardy casino player at Atlantic City's Tropicana on a dreaded Friday the 13th went along with the gag and played slot machine No. 1313. You guessed it—he hit a million-dollar-plus jackpot on the No. 1313 machine. I would guess that from that day on, he looked forward to Friday the 13th even more than his birthday.

Everyone has read about someone who had a sudden stroke of luck, when lightning strikes and "it" happened. Maybe the next time it can happen to you.

Did it ever happen that some oddball circumstance, not planned, and not of my making, turned into a "lucky" twist of fate at the tables for me? Occasionally, yes. One instance I vividly recall was an episode at the Frontier in Las Vegas in the 1970s. I was back-to-back at blackjack tables with my weekend date. I was at a $25-minimum table, backed up to her at a $5 table. The lady shied away from sitting with me, as my comparatively high-stake playing made her too nervous. Frankly I was glad she was at another table, as her being nervous would only have made me nervous.

My dealer was a speed demon. Man, was he fast! After betting $250 and winning, I turned my head for what seemed to me to be a split-second, just to ask my gal a question before picking up my chips and making another bet. When I turned back to the table, my $250 bet, along with my $250 winnings, were in play, and Speedy was in the midst of dealing the hand. Before I had a chance to cry foul, my eyes popped out of my head as I gazed down upon a beautiful Queen of Hearts, topped off with a handsome Ace of Spades, for $750 payoff for my "mistake" $500 bet.

Sure, I won big on this comedy of errors, but it could have easily turned into a tragedy of errors, and washed away the $500 that I had no intention of wagering. The lesson to be learned here is to stay alert, and keep your eye at all times on your money on the table. Don't depend on luck, or dumb luck, to help you come home with some of the casino's money.

Sixth Sense

I don't believe in voodoo mumbo-jumbo, but I do believe there is such a thing as ESP—extrasensory perception—especially if you spend enough years surfing the casinos. I've experienced it myself a number of times. I can't explain how or why; I can only tell you that it happened to me. It happened also to a gal from Sacramento, California, who had a sudden premonition that she was going to hit it big on a slot machine and, over the protestations of her family, drove all night from Sacramento to Reno. As the *National Enquirer* reported it in a splashy picture story, she marched up to a quarter progressive machine and promptly hit for over a million.

It also happened to Allan J. Wilson, a publishing executive from New York. As he relates it, he was at a craps table in Las Vegas when he had a premonition that the shooter would have a great roll. Confidently, he wagered heavily, backing his bets up all the way. The shooter held the dice for thirty-eight minutes!

There have been times when the dice were in the air and I *knew* what the outcome would be. More than once I started to walk away from the craps table before the dice landed and the stickman announced, "Seven and out." And there were times I confidently relaxed at my place at the table, just waiting for my bet to be paid off before the shooter even finished his "windup," preparing to toss the dice down the way.

A friend, who asked not to be named, has a special prescience. I've seen him in action in both Las Vegas and Atlantic City, where he would announce to everyone at the craps table, "This time I'm going to throw a five" . . .and damned if he didn't throw that five. Or, he'd toss the cubes over his shoulder and predict a nine, etc.

One particular roll I vividly remember was at the Desert Inn, where he announced a hard eight *and got it.*

I'm not the only one who noted his prescience at the gambling tables. Brad Darrah, a reporter, wrote an eight-page feature article in *Life* Magazine on this friend, where Darrah made the incredible assertion that he actually saw an *aura* emanating from the man as he rolled the dice in Caesars Palace! A most remarkable occurrence, if true, and also remarkable is the fact that *Life* would even print it!

So, don't be surprised, if you are a casino habitué for long enough, you start getting "that feeling. . . ."

Tales of Luck and Folly

The record for holding the dice goes to Stanley Fujitake from Hawaii, who in July, 1989 at Las Vegas' downtown California Club held the dice for an incredible three-hours-and-twelve minutes! By the time he sevened out the table had paid out almost a million dollars.

♠ ♠ ♠ ♠ ♠

When "Mrs. Lucky" (she opted to remain anonymous) hit that long-overdue Megabucks World's Record jackpot of $27,582,539 on November 15, 1998 at Vegas' Palace Station Casino, she truly beat the slot machine odds in cards and spades. Only a paltry nickel out of every dollar fed into the machines is ever earmarked for the jackpot. That meant over *half-a-billion dollars* had to have been pumped into the Megabucks machines all across Nevada to have funded Mrs. Lucky's multi-million-dollar windfall. But that's not the end of the story. When you're lucky, you're just lucky. Only a month prior to her Megabucks win, Mrs. Lucky had hit a Wheel of Fortune slot machine jackpot for more than $680,000!

♠ ♠ ♠ ♠ ♠

Dr. Joseph Damato, a dentist from Newark, New Jersey, visited what was then the Grand in Atlantic City in 1992 to enter a blackjack tournament. Luck wasn't with him when he discovered that then, of all times, he had lost his glasses.

Afraid to enter the tournament because, as he put it, "I couldn't see the cards so well," he decided to wile away the afternoon by playing the Megabucks slot machine, the symbols of which were easier for him to see. And luck rebounded in a Megabucks blast as the dentist drilled into a $4,400,000 Megabucks jackpot.

♠ ♠ ♠ ♠ ♠

Flukes, blunders, and just plain dumb luck (as you know, I don't believe in "luck," but I'll take it if it happens) have enabled me to win and to lose through the years. The $400 in $100 bills that I found in an Atlantic City taxicab one Christmas week falls in the "easy-money-dumb-luck" category. Ditto for the $200 in $50 bills I found on the floor of a stall in a Caesars Palace men's room.

The Caesars windfall was just a bunch of bills folded in half; the cab jackpot was in a small Christmas money envelope along with a card: "For Tony. Good luck from Al." If it wasn't for bad luck, Tony wouldn't have any luck at all; poor Tony lost Al's bonus money in Atlantic City before he even put his toe in a casino.

Then there was the time at a $25 table when I inadvertently

won an extra $475 on a hand. I carelessly buried a $500 chip under a lowly $25 chip; I meant it only as a $50 bet. The dealer, asleep at the switch, should have noted "purple action" to alert the pit boss that money played. I won the hand and happily learned at the payoff that I had more riding on the wager than I had intended.

But, alas, I lost the $475 back, on another day, plus an extra $25. It was on a chaotic Fourth of July at the Trump Plaza. The joint was jumping, with the aisles as packed with people as the Times Square subway station is at rush hour. Having won a tidy sum, I arose from the blackjack table with my hands piled high with chips of all kinds. I neglected to call "color in" and change my smaller-denomination chips before backing into the surging crowds. You can guess what happened next. Overloaded, I was jostled by some goon, which caused me to drop a chip under the feet of the mass of moving mankind. A purple chip, no less—worth $500!

I sadly surveyed the mob scene all around me and instantly, painfully decided to just write it off. Recovering the chip would have necessitated causing an uproar in the casino. They would have had to call in security guards to halt the moving mob of people and to clear the immense crowd in the aisle to make the space for me so I could look for my chip. Five hundred dollars is a lot of money for anyone to lose but, in this situation, it wasn't worth the grief. If I could go back and do it again, I'd make the same decision. My consolation was imagining the thrill someone in the casino experienced when he or she found my $500 chip. I hope it was some poor slob who never even found a $5 bill in his life.

My next move was to go back to the seat I had just vacated to try to win back the lost purple chip. And I did! But I lost it back gambling at the tables at the next casino.

Call it a fluke, a coincidence, or a freak occurrence, but here's what happened when I arrived in Las Vegas with a girl who had never been there before. She was eager to explore Circus Circus.

So there we were, strolling the sideshow exhibits, where we were amused by a cute little monkey attraction. I handed the little fellow in the cage a five-dollar token, whereupon he went into a cute little dance, and then handed me a card with a fortune. My fortune that day? "Go home. Today's not your lucky day."

We should have followed the monkey's sage advice and hightailed it out of town on the next plane. Not only did I lose my proverbial shirt on that ill-fated Vegas trip, but my pants and underwear went along too.

If you spend enough time in casinos you'll have your share of flukes and blunders. Some work in your favor, some don't. Chalk it up to casino adventure and take it all in stride.

In Atlantic City, Trump Plaza was another story. When the old bus terminal was still in operation, the closest casino was Trump Plaza. Every time my wife Stella and I went for a day at the seashore (we never stayed overnight) my standard-order-of-procedure was to meander over to the Boardwalk entrance of the Plaza. While Stella sunned herself on a bench outside, I'd make my initial foray inside, with a modest goal of winning a hundred dollars of "mad money" for her. Maybe it was my fresh enthusiasm in hitting the first casino of the day, or perhaps it was my mega-positive attitude, but damned if I didn't return to Stella on the Boardwalk most of the time with Donald Trump's money.

Sure, there were times The Donald nailed me, some of which I blame solely on myself.

Now pay attention while I teach you a lesson I learned the hard, expensive way. Never, but never gamble when you're in an ugly mood. If you are mad at somebody or something, in a temper tantrum or a blind rage, you're not in control of all your faculties. You risk doing damn foolish things at the tables, which I invariable did when I was in such an ugly mood.

If you're engulfed in some sour situation, do yourself a favor and go to the movies or take a long walk on the boardwalk; just steer clear of the table games! If there isn't a movie house close by, or it's too rainy to promenade on the boardwalk, then cut your losses by playing the nickel slot machine. Yes, Atlantic City casinos have nickel slots. I believe these were originally mandated by the Casino Control Commission to make sure that the Little People—the Low Rollers—can gamble and have a little fun there, too.

Let me tell you about one fiasco. In Atlantic City—coming off an ongoing argument that had started in our apartment and continued onto the bus and all the way up to Stella's Boardwalk bench in front of the Plaza—I charged into the casino in a murderous mood. Gambling with real money, I had a lethal combination that spells guaranteed financial disaster. This time it was really "mad" money, but the term took on an entirely different meaning. In my blind rage I literally pissed away more than $6,000 of my bankroll, a staggering loss that I couldn't overcome at the other casinos. Let me spell it out for you one more time: NEVER GAMBLE WHEN YOU'RE IN A BAD MOOD.

♠ ♠ ♠ ♠ ♠

A good boxman at the craps tables has sharper eyes than an eagle, and is ten times more street savvy than a sidewalk peddler in front of Macy's. He is always on the alert for unusual moves by a player, especially the person shooting the dice. More than once I have seen the boxman halt the game and request that the player holding the dice—particularly if he switched them from one hand to the other, or made some other unorthodox movement with the cubes—to drop them back on the table for examination before allowing them to be put back into play.

Any die that flies off the table is returned to the boxman to be checked before the shooter can continue the roll. Dice in play at each table are secretly coded to prevent any loaded dice from being switched into the game. Only once did I see a die fly off the table and get returned directly into play without the boxman examining it. The player who picked up the cube and directly tossed it back into action for the shooter was Dean Martin.

When a die, or both dice, are thrown with such force that they fly off the craps table, great care is taken to find the cube or cubes and return it, or them, to the boxman. Sometimes a game can be halted for several minutes while players, stickmen, and pit personnel scurry around looking for the lost dice.

One time a die whizzed past me and, no matter how hard we all looked, the cube never showed up. Later, at a blackjack table, I reached into my jacket pocket for a Kleenex and came up with the missing die.

I've heard stories of loaded dice being switched into the game. If true, this had to be done with the contrivance of both the boxman and the stickmen, if not the pit boss too. With all the safeguards in place in today's casinos it would be a daring and risky undertaking.

Some boxmen have a sixth sense when it comes to the roll of the dice. Ask me, I know. The simple movement of the index finger of a boxman at the Las Vegas Sands during my wild and foolhardy early days foraying in the casinos cost me thousands of dollars. That one little movement by the boxman's index finger at the Sands cost me $6,500. It also sounded the death-knell for one of my first ill-conceived hotshot, sure-fire "systems."

Even today I wince at my daring, and the ultimate disastrous consequences of that system. Rather than relating the painful details myself, here's how my mentor, Lyle Stuart, told it in his *Winning at Casino Gambling*:

"[A] postscript about my friend, Arnold. On one occasion he believed he had a sure-fire system. He would stand at a craps table, wait for the shooter to come out with a point and then place bets of $1,000 on the 5 and 9, $1,200 each on the 6 and 8, and he'd buy the 4 and 10 for $1,000 each.

"This put him at risk for $6,500, including the vig (vigorish or tribute) on the 4 and 10. On the next roll of the dice, if the shooter made his point or *any* of the other five numbers, Arnold would collect his winnings, take down all his wagers, and walk away.

"He went from casino-to-casino. He came home several thousand dollars ahead.

"'Arnold,' I said, 'that's no system except for suicide! You can't overcome dice odds that way!'

"Did you ever talk to a brick wall?

"Arnold smiled benignly at me. What did I know?

"All he knew was that he went back to Las Vegas and won again. And again. . . .

"[H]e made another journey to his easy-money land. This trip didn't begin well. He walked up to a table, waited until the shooter threw a point, then made his $6,500 worth of bets. The next roll was a seven.

"He hurried to another table and did the same thing. The second roll was a 7. After it happened at the third table in the casino, he stumbled across the Strip to another casino [the Sands]. It happened three times again. He came home a $39,000 loser.

"Neither of us ever mentioned his 'system' again."

Now let me fill you in on all the gory details of my Last Stand at that ill-chosen craps table at the Sands. . . .

Early on, I did have success with my One-Roll "System." Then, on that most unfortunate day, after I already had lost five times in a row, I convinced myself it just couldn't happen for a sixth time. No way. This time would be a sure-thing winner.

I bellied-up to the next craps table and saw that 8 was the point. Couldn't be better. In a loud voice I confidently announced "$6,500, across the board," dropping the necessary chips onto the cloth. As always, a bet of this size aroused the attention of both the table personnel and the players. The boxman peered at me intently. I could see that he was sizing me up. Me, I couldn't have cared less but, in retrospect, I should have cared more. Somehow, instinctively, he had my number.

A gaunt cowboy at the end of the table was the shooter. Now the dice were set on the cloth in front of the boxman, ready for the next roll. Then the boxman did a curious thing. With his right index finger he turned over one of the dice, just gave it one little turn. Then the stickman pushed the dice over to the shooter, who picked them up and threw them against the back wall for a 7-out. The boxman flashed a broad smile and snapped his fingers with an "I-knew-I-did-it" flourish. And damned if he didn't. That single roll retired my "one-roll-system" for good.

As I gambled more in the casinos I learned more, a lot more. Perhaps my ill-fated "one-roll-at-a-table-hit-and-run system" will teach you what *not* to do in the casinos. In theory it was a good system. In practice it was a road to ruin.

Gambler's Potpourri

✓ OTB
✓ Video Poker
✓ Keno
✓ Roulette

OTB

I've gone into an Off-Track Betting (OTB) parlor about a dozen times in my life, eleven times to duck into the doorway to get out of the rain, and once—just once—to place a bet. That one time that I *did* bet, I won, making me probably the only guy in New York City who can say that he has bet at OTB and quit winners.

That one isolated OTB incident happened because my wife Stella's sister and brother-in-law came into the city to have lunch with us in Chinatown, right next door to an OTB parlor. Having never been in a legal bookmaking joint, they were hot to place a bet or two. I figured what the hell, I'm already here so I might as well go along with the crowd and put my two bucks down too. Knowing zip about the horses, I decided to consult the people who claim to have the inside track on the nags—the handicappers who pick 'em for the tabloids. Fishing in the trash cans I found their daily tout sheets. Almost all of the pony pundits had concurred, first, that a couple of the nags would come in first and second in the first race, an "exacta." As they obviously knew more about these particular horses than I did, I went along with their picks. I won $54 for my two bucks, which made me The Last of the Big-Time Spenders with my in-laws, as I treated everyone to Chinese lunch with my windfall.

Video Poker

Time magazine had a most informative article on the video poker machines in South Carolina.

The state has more than 30,000 of these machines in operation, each one of which earns a yearly net profit of $22,000. (I can't help wondering how many South Carolinians have incomes of *less* than $22,000.)

♠ ♠ ♠ ♠ ♠

While the Nevada casinos have installed $500 and $1,000 slot machines, they also have reverted to the other end of the spectrum with the reintroduction of penny slots. Most notable are the penny video poker machines with their impressive 98% payback. Novice slot machine players can both, at the same time, learn as well as enjoy the game with an optimum five-coin investment (a nickel!) where the best pay-off schedules are. No, pennies aren't showered into the coin trough when you win; paper vouchers are dispensed as cash-outs, which you can take over to the coin cashier for folding money.

As impressive as is the 98% payback of these penny video poker machines, the Las Vegas Stratosphere Casino advertised a 100% guaranteed payback on their dollar video poker machines. Anything to bring 'em into the joint.

Bingo

Before the proliferation of casinos, except for the occasional church "Las Vegas Night," Bingo was the only game in town where you could legally gamble for money. Today, Bingo in the casinos is small potatoes compared to the slot machines and table games, yet years ago in some locales, Bingo was a very lucrative enterprise. Even Steve Wynn had his beginnings running Bingo games in Maryland.

Today, outside of casinos, the game is still a small-time operation, run by church and civic organizations. But not so when "The Boys" decide to put their collective beefy toes inside the church's Bingo Hall door.

Such was the case, according to the May 14, 1998 *Catholic News*, when the Staten Island, New York Vice Squad stormed into St. Christopher parochial school and arrested five people for bookmaking. The bookies had already arranged a staggering $16,000 in illegal side bets from just one hundred or so players!

"I'm so glad it happened," the Catholic weekly quoted Monsignor Kenneth A. Gerathy, the pastor of the parochial school. "We've been trying to stop this for some time."

Maybe the Monsignor was glad it happened but, according to Gersh Kuntzman in his following Sunday's column in the *New York Post*, almost nobody else in the Bingo Hall was.

"Tell the bookies we miss them," said Mary Owens, a regular at the Sunday and Monday games at St. Christopher's. "It's boring without them."

According to the columnist, Ms. Owen's sentiments were echoed by most of the senior citizens at the first post-bust Bingo session. It was, in fact, the parish that had tipped off the cops in the first place—that precipitated the Vice Squad raid at the parochial school.

Why?

The good Fathers had good reasons why. As the *New York Post* put it, "There was just too much money being made by the bookies, and too little taken in by the church." But all that will be rectified. "The church is now planning to be its own bookie, hoping to accept 'line' bets if the state and city give it a permit."

Bingo is far from the best bang for your buck in the casino, but it can be a relaxing way to pass an occasional lazy afternoon playing the game, so go to it, pal, and I hope you have a bonanza of Bingos.

Keno

In most casinos today Keno is an electronic, computer-fed game. Twenty numbers out of a pool of eighty are zapped with machine-gun rapidity onto huge electronic screens on the sides of the casino.

Keno wasn't always played this way. Up until the 1990s it was a manually operated game, with the eighty numbered ping-pong balls in a transparent fishbowl-shaped container. Two rabbit-ear-shaped transparent tubes stuck out on top, and ten balls were air-blown into each. The whole operation was up front and visible to all the players in the Keno Lounge. No mysterious numbers shooting out of the blue onto electronic wall boards.

It was during the late 70s that I got a bug up my ass to investigate this oddball casino game that offered a $25,000 payoff for a buck investment. At the tail-end of a flying weekend, I had lots of time to spare before my flight home. Plunking myself down in the Sahara's Keno Lounge, mostly as a time-killer, I reached over to the nearest trash can and fished out the cover sheets of the last dozen or so games. (See illustration.)

I tallied all the winning numbers, game-by-game, curious to see if there was any pattern to the drawn numbers. As soon as I finished the tally, I ordered a bottle of beer and examined what I had.

What I saw before me really got my attention. Some Keno numbers repeated regularly, while other numbers never came up at all! Now I was interested. I went back to the trash can and tallied in the four games that were played while I was doing my paper-work, which brought me up-to-date.

CAESARS
ATLANTIC CITY
$250,000 KENO
LIMIT EACH GAME TO AGGREGATE PLAYERS

No. Of Games: **2**   Total Price All Games: **6⁻**

1	2	3	4	5	6	7	⊗	⊗	10
11	12	13	14	⊗	⊗	17	18	19	20
21	22	23	24	25	26	27	28	29	30
31	32	33	34	35	36	37	38	39	40

Price Per Game: **3⁻**   1/8 $1⁻

PAY ON COMPUTER GENERATED TICKETS ONLY

41	42	43	44	45	46	47	48	⊗	⊗
51	52	53	54	55	56	57	58	59	60
61	62	⊗	64	65	66	67	68	69	70
71	72	73	⊗	75	76	77	78	79	80

$.50   4/2

SHOWBOAT
PLAY KENO

$7   1 / 7

Mark Ways And Price: 3/2   3/4   1/6   @   1.-

1	⊗	3	4	5	6	7	8	9	10
11	12	⊗	14	15	16	17	18	19	20
21	22	23	24	25	26	27	28	29	30
31	32	33	34	35	36	37	38	39	40

Your wager is represented only by the computer-generated ticket issued to you

41	42	43	44	45	46	47	48	49	50
51	52	53	54	⊗	56	57	58	59	60
61	62	63	64	⊗	66	67	68	⊗	70
71	72	73	74	75	76	77	78	⊗	80

Actually I had some advance knowledge of the potential of Keno. Once, years ago, when a friend's son was too young to enter a Las Vegas casino, he sat in the lobby, spending his time keeping track of the Keno board above the hotel registration desk. When his father came by, the son mentioned to him that certain numbers were repeating. The father invested $22.50 in variations of the numbers. Not one came up on the next game. Not discouraged he repeated the bets. The second time around, the 12-year-old won $2,500.

How could I have been so blind as to ignore Keno all these years? A Keno regular tipped me off that the 8-spot was the best bet for the money. So I went over to the Keno counter, where games go on every fifteen minutes or so, and bet twenty-five 8-spot games at a buck each. When the game was over, to my delight I found that I had won $260 on my investment of twenty-five bucks.

I pocketed the windfall and decided then and there that on my next Vegas visit I would play Keno exclusively.

Ten days later I returned to Las Vegas, and the Sahara.

Once in my room, I unpacked my working tools: an accountant's yellow pad, a ruler, and a fine-line accountant's pen that I had purchased especially for the trip. Off to the Keno Lounge, where I zeroed in on the trash cans toward the back, and fished out all the discarded cover sheets from the previously played games. I sorted them out, amassing a complete set of the past 26 games.

Now I was ready.

I set to work on the tedious job of tracking the winning numbers of all 26 games on my yellow-lined accountant's pad. Thirty minutes later I had it all down. I went back to the trash can to retrieve and tally the games played since.

Now I had all the information I needed. It was time to play Keno for keeps. If I was serious in my endeavor, it meant that I should play Keno on steady a basis. I couldn't just play a couple cards at a time.

I played one hundred 8-spot games at a buck a game, every game. I played and I tallied. And I played and I tallied. And I played and I tallied. For sixteen straight hours, nonstop, I played the game and then tallied it onto my sheet. To keep my wits about me, I eschewed alcohol and lived solely on coffee frosteds and tomato juice, which, from time-to-time necessitated rapid, punctuated trips to the nearest men's room to run some water through my lingam.

When the smoke cleared sixteen hours and thousands of games later, did I ever get an eight-out-of-eight and make that $25,000 windfall?

The answer is no.

Did I win or did I lose during my Keno marathon? Again, the answer is no to *both* questions.

Okay, let me explain.

Keno is like a greased pig—you almost have it, but, dammit, the oily porker always slips out of your clutches. There were times during the sixteen-hour marathon when I was two or three thousand ahead, only to hit a dry spell where everything evened out, and even dipped into the minus column. During my 16-hour marathon I had a 7-out-of-8 in the first ten numbers picked, only to be zeroed out in the next ten numbers. All I needed was one number out of the second ten, just one more goddam number, but it never did show up.

The Keno writers worked on six-hour shifts; six hours on and twelve off. As I was on a sixteen-hour marathon, just before I was ready to call it a day, the first shift returned. "Oh, I see you're back," commented a Keno writer as he marked up my tickets.

"I never left," I told him.

He peered at me intently for a moment, then muttered, "Buddy, you're bulletproof."

When, bowing to sheer exhaustion, I packed it in at the end of the sixteen-hour marathon session, I was about $600 ahead—a $600 profit for playing almost 15,000 games! Without a doubt, it was the hardest $600 I ever made, gambling or otherwise. I blindly stumbled out of the Keno Lounge down the hall to my hotel room. Once in my room, I was afraid to take a bath in my zombie-like condition; I feared I'd drown in the tub! Instead I staggered into the shower. Once under the soothing warm water I closed my eyes—just for a second—and fell asleep standing up! I only know this because as I slumped against the shower wall I was jarred awake by my own snoring! Needless to add, I was forever cured from playing Keno.

Postscript: Is the game completely honest? I can only answer that in regard to an episode during my Marathon Monday sixteen-hour session at the Sahara. Counting the spots on one of my tickets, I found I had a 6-out-of-8, an $1,100 winner. When I handed in my ticket, the manager of the Keno table came over to me and informed me that my ticket was mismarked and incorrect, and that they only pay on the *original* ticket, which was locked away during the game. Of course I was ready for a fight, but before I could say anything he pointed to my original ticket, which had 7-out-of-8, a $2,200 *winner!*

Roulette

When I think of roulette, I think of three varieties of the game—one European, and two American.

Of the three, the European version presents the best chance for the player. There is only one zero on the layout, and on certain bets, if the little white ball happens to land in the zero slot, the player has an option to save part of his bet *en prison.*

There is a world of difference between the two American versions. One version also has the single zero, but unlike its European cousin, in this game if the zero comes up, and you didn't bet on zero, you lose. Period. The second version has a layout with both a zero AND a double-zero, and is a flat-out rip-off. I urge you to avoid wasting your money there.

It amazes me that, when casinos have *both* zero and double-zero roulette tables, as is the case with the Monte Carlo in Las Vegas, *both* tables are busy. That's why casino owners never overestimate the intelligence of their players.

Of all the games in the casino, none has inspired more "systems" devised to guarantee victory than roulette. The most famous—or infamous—is the Martingale, where the player doubles his bet after each loss, relying on the certainty of eventually having a winning spin. The fatal flaw in this "system" is the built-in table betting limit, which prevents unlimited doubling-up. Even without a table betting limit, the Martingale system remains faulty. There is no guarantee, even if you wager on Red 99 times in a row, that on the hundredth spin Red will show up.

The little white ball, like the dice on the craps table, has no memory. I learned this axiom the very hard way in London, when I brashly aimed to win a few pounds to buy a bauble for a lady friend, and threw my chips on Red. Spin-after-spin, Black came up, until I reached the table limit and had to stop. I retreated from the table like a beaten dog. I felt I had lost enough money on this Martingale sham to buy an interest in the British crown jewels. Needless to mention, I never tried that "foolproof" system again.

I won't go into all the nuances and nitty-gritties of the game of roulette. If you're still hell-bent to play it, there are plenty of gambling how-to books available. The only person I know of who had a rational game plan for a go at roulette, and was determined to put it into operation if he could, was a dealer from a London casino who had saved up the equivalent of $200,000.

He wrote to all the casinos in Las Vegas, challenging them to take his *one* $200,000 bet on just *one* spin of the roulette wheel, wagering on a color. Many of the casinos declined, a few offered to take him on, but only in a series of bets. Only Binion's accepted his challenge.

The Britisher came across the Atlantic with his wagering money, and prepared for the One Big Spin. Red was his choice of color. English gentleman that he was, he came to the casino decked out in a tuxedo.

The double-zero slot was closed off, and the Englishman gave the wheel a few practice spins. Finally, he nodded, and told Binion, "this is going to be it." A dealer gave the wheel a good healthy "push," and around and around went the little white ball, popping at last into a neat little red niche. The Britisher collected his winnings and returned to Jolly Old England, $200,000 richer (minus what taxes the Infernal Revenue Service was able to siphon off).

This was not the only daring bet in Binion's history. Binion's was known for going-for-broke wagers. At Binion's you could make your first big bet your gambling limit. One time a seedy-looking character in a bulky old overcoat was shooting craps at a $5 table when Binion walked by. "What's my limit?" croaked the geezer.

"The sky's the limit for you, Pop," was Binion's jocular reply. Immediately the guy started emptying out all the pockets of his voluminous clothing until there was a mountain of bills in front of him!

A legendary episode was played out over a decade ago when Jack Binion got a phone call from a man who wanted to know how high a wager he would accept. "One million if it's your first bet," Jack told him. A few days later a middle-aged cowboy arrived with two shopping bags filled with money. It was poured onto the green felt table and counted. It came to $760,000.

"Give me one chip," he said.

He placed the chip on the "don't pass" line.

A shooter threw dice in something like this sequence: 6-4-12-9, and finally a 7 and out.

The casino counted out $1,520,000, and Jack Binion gave the player two attache cases filled with money.

As the unidentified man left the casino accompanied by two armed security guards, someone asked him, "Why did you do it?"

"Well," he drawled, "I felt inflation was shrinking my savings, so I decided to gamble on double or nothing."

Alas, that wasn't the end of the story. Within the year he returned and lost most of it back. Later there was a report that the man committed suicide.

Finally, *The High Roller* reported that a Richard Jarecki of Heidelberg won more than $50,000 at roulette at the San Remo Casino over a seven-month period. The City Council tried to ban him as a "professional gambler," but the German took some of his winnings and hired two Italian lawyers, who successfully forced the Council to rescind the ban. His point was that, if both he and the Casino are honest, the odds are against him anyway. Back to the roulette table he went, and out he came—a winner again.

Slots And Table Games

✓ Slots and the IRS

✓ Slot Statistics

✓ Table Game Statistics

Slots and the IRS

As I mentioned earlier, in my decades of slot action, I did hit one $5,000 jackpot. I wasn't even trying for a big win; I was just hoping for cab fare to the next casino. As it happened, this was during my early casino life when I wasn't very savvy, so I filled out the required W-2 form for gambling winnings and paid the appropriate taxes due on April 15. (Any machine winnings of $1,200 or more are taxable. Many casinos legally circumvent the regulation by having slot machines and Keno tickets pay out $1,199.)

To see the total unfairness of the federal gambling tax setup, consider that only the poor man's games are targeted: Keno, Bingo, the slot machines. High Rollers who wager thousands of dollars or more on the turn of a card can win a king's ransom at the tables and are not required to fill out any tax forms as long as they don't cash in more than $10,000 in any 24-hour period.

Not everyone plays by IRS rules when it comes to W-2G taxes. A friend of mine (I'll call him Tom) told me how he beat the system. Tom hit a quarter progressive machine at the Desert Inn in Vegas for $10,000. Bells went off and the machine started humming with a steady, annoying drone. Over the loudspeaker it was announced that machine number so-and-so had hit a $10,000 jackpot.

A shift manager with a clipboard arrived, as did a slot machine mechanic, who opened the machine and carefully checked it out.

Another casino honcho showed with a camera and took Tom's picture.

Tom quipped that he initially thought it was because he was such a handsome guy. Later he found out the photo was taken to compare his face with photos in a Rogue's Gallery of slot machine cheats.

The bells continued to ring and the buzz was still buzzing. Next, a burly security guard with a clipboard showed up and gave Tom a W-2G federal tax form to fill out. Leaning on a vacant blackjack table nearby, the goon also asked for and carefully checked Tom's driver's license, Social Security card, and a credit card to verify that Tom was indeed Tom.

Totally pissed off (with the ringing and the buzzer still buzzing), Tom, who originally intended to take his winnings in cash, announced that he wanted a *check* for his $10,000. The shift manager wasn't happy about that, for the casino's hope and expectation was that Tom would drop much of his winnings back into the slots.

Tom got his check and departed the casino. Two nights later he was dining with his girl friend at the Four Queens downtown when it suddenly dawned on him that he was doing it *all wrong*. They quickly finished their meal and he took a taxi back to the Desert Inn. There Tom passed the check into the cashier's cage and requested credit at the tables for the full amount. From table-to-table Tom and his lady went—blackjack, craps, roulette—every time signing markers for credit against his $10,000 check at the tables, all the while accumulating chips. Gambling ostentatiously, but in reality betting small, Tom kept slipping chips to his lady, who shuttled back-and-forth from the tables, cashing them in. When April 15 came around, along with his copy of the casino's W-2G tax form for his $10,000 win, Tom attached Xeroxes of $12,000 in markers. (To buffer his deductions, during the course of the evening he deposited with the cashier another $2,000 in cash for additional credit at the tables.)

The Bottom Line: Won $10,000. Lost $12,000.

Total gambling tax liability: zero (The IRS will allow you to deduct losses only up to your documented winnings, but not a cent more.)

Xeroxes of casino markers are not the only way to prove you were a loser in the casinos. Any gambling losses you can show are applicable against your casino, lottery, or racetrack winnings. The Internal Revenue Service lumps all forms of gambling together, except for the stock market. (Nicolas Darvas once wrote a book entitled *Wall Street: The Other Las Vegas*.)

In the casino, the only gambling "receipts" available to the player are losing Keno tickets. Of course, you can keep a diary of where you played, what you played, and what you won and lost, but that's a monstrous pain in the ass, and tends to take the fun out of gambling. If you are fortunate enough to win big, and you need proof of gambling losses, the Keno trash cans are a good starting point. Just make sure your Keno tickets don't have coffee stains and cigarette burns. The race track and Off-Track Betting parlors are two other places to collect losing tickets. Be sure that tickets from the race track and betting parlors don't have heel marks. In case of an audit, IRS agents actually check your boxes of losing tickets for any tell-tale heel marks!

♠ ♠ ♠ ♠ ♠

Almost everyone today knows about the random number enumerator microchips that controls slot machine payouts, but few know that changing the chip on the "hit" frequency—which can vary from 1 percent to 15 percent—is fairly simple. It's akin to changing the fuse in your fuse box at home. In Nevada, casinos can change RNE chips at will without notifying the Casino Control Board, as long as the new chips were previously approved.

The good news is that the casinos *cannot* change the frequency on either the video poker or video blackjack machines.

♠ ♠ ♠ ♠ ♠

At one time it was a Federal offense to ship slot machines across state lines into states that banned them as illegal. This is no longer so. In fact, you can legally own an antique slot machine for your den or rumpus room. Check "Coin Machines" in your Yellow Pages to find your friendly local slot machine dealer.

♠ ♠ ♠ ♠ ♠

When I was a kid in Brooklyn, there used to be a candy store on every block. Now, in California, Proposition 5 passed, and now all one-hundred-and-one—that's right, a hundred-and-one—Indian tribes are eligible to open casinos up and down the state.

A California gambler will feel like a kid on a block full of candy stores. The Governor strongly opposed video slot machines but, according to the Associated Press, he is now amenable to "an electronic lottery machine that spits out a series of numbers on a slip of paper, rather than dumping coins." Talk about hypocritical bullshit . . .

Slot Statistics

Someone once said there are three kinds of lies: lies, damn lies, and statistics.

Consider this:

What a wonderful country America is, where more than 91 percent of American homes have indoor plumbing!

Now try this:

What a disgrace to our nation, that with our booming economy and all our wealth and natural resources, 9 percent of our American homes all lack the bare necessity of indoor plumbing!

The same figure, twisted two different ways. (These figures in my example here are not accurate. I just took some numbers off the top of my head to illustrate how statistics can be manipulated.) There are, however, casino statistics that can prove valuable to you, especially with respect to *where* you can play the slot machines.

Compiled by the New Jersey Casino Control Commission are the slot statistics, from the nickle machines all the way up to the $100 machines.

If you track the statistics, as I do, you come up with some eye-opening—and sometimes eye-popping—figures.

New Jersey magazine had it in every issue. Tracking the statistics for six months in a row, from October 1997 through March 1998, I came up with some interesting data. Two casinos shared the honors of having the loosest slots over-all, with three monthly "wins" each: The Tropicana on the Boardwalk, and Harrah's on the Marina.

For *all* of the six months tracked, the Trop had the highest payouts on the 25¢ machines, which are the most popular slots in the casinos. For the nickel-machine player, the Claridge was top dog, leading the pack for five-of-the-six-months tracked.

Ten of the twelve casinos have from three to nine $100 machines each. The Claridge is the only casino without any $100 slots, and the Showboat is the only casino with just one. Las Vegas casinos really cater to these high roller players with both $500 and $1,000 slot machines.

The eye-popping statistics for the six months I tracked were on the hundred-dollar slot machine at the Showboat casino. Frankly, if these figures hadn't come from the Commission, I would be skeptical. Here goes:

October 1997	190.3%
November 1997	112.2%
December 1997	162.7%
January 1998	61.5%
February 1998	117.3%
March 1998	95.9%

For four-of-the-six-months, the Showboat's lone $100 machine was a horn of plenty for the players who pumped their dollars into it. The party came to a screeching halt in April 1998, when the machine suddenly tightened up, producing an incredibly low payout of only 10.1 percent, probably the lowest payout of *any* machine in the history of Atlantic City's legalized gambling. I was so incredulous over the 10.1 percent figure that I wrote to the Casino Control Commission for verification, which I received.

It is interesting to note that the Claridge, the casino that led the pack in lavish payouts on the nickel machine, was the last casino in *overall* percentage of payouts. So, on the basis of this six-month mini-survey, if you're a 5¢ slot player, the Claridge casino is the place for you. If, however, you're playing the machines taking coin denominations from a quarter up, you'd do well to play anywhere but the Claridge. I'm sure that the savvy $100-machine players who had access to these figures all flocked to the Showboat's $100 machine.

As I pointed out earlier, slot machines are the cash-cows for any casino. On a steady basis, slots show more profit than the table games. If you must invest your money in the slots, I urge you to subscribe to *Casino Player* magazine so that you can get an idea of which casinos will give you the most bang for your buck.

Slot percentage guides are important for slot machine players, as they allow them to zero in on the casinos with the "loosest" machines in their choice of coin denomination.

The Casino Control Commission also issues monthly a *New*

Jersey Casino Industry Financial Report, this is a thirty-page disclosure document that breaks down the profit-and-loss statistics on every slot machine denomination and every table game, as reported to the Commission by each casino. It's dull but useful to read, as the thirty pages are nothing more than just one dry sheet of statistics after another.

Looking over the huge maze of figures in one report, with literally thousands of listed entries, I was curious to see what I could learn. I charted the statistics regarding slot machines and table games.

It was a painstakingly slow job, but when I finally finished and saw what I had in front of me, I was more than repaid for my labors. I now had in front of me *all* the background data on *all* the machines and *all* the table games in *all* the casinos.

I found out important information about the slot machines, including how much money each casino made on each denomination machine, and even how many of each kind was on the casino floor. (To my surprise, the wild roller-coaster ride on the $100 slots at the Showboat was for just *one* machine!)

This is what I learned from my slot machine charting, probably the first time this information has ever been laid out for the gambler in a book on Atlantic City casinos. I am reprinting my charts, as is.

The quarter machine was the big winner for *all* the casinos, with six of the twelve casinos netting more than $10 million each for the month. None of the other six cleared less than $6 million on these cash-cow machines.

Percentage wise, outside of the lowly nickel machine, the quarter slots gave the casinos their biggest bite of the player's dollar.

Surprisingly, the least profitable of all were the $100 slots, with only one casino netting as much as $263,000 on them for the month. (Resorts even lost $52,000 that month on their $100 machines.)

The $25 slots were more profitable for the casinos than their

CASINO	5¢	WIN/LOSS	25¢	WIN	50¢	WIN	$1	WIN
Hilton	11.5%	194K	9.6%	6.7M	9.2%	1.37M	8.7%	2.83M
Bally's	10.6%	1.1M	9.4%	15.1M	8.0%	2.97M	8.3%	6.0M
Caesars	NA	NA	9.7%	9.1M	8.2%	2.7M	7.7%	4.3M
Claridge	7.4%	109K	9.1%	6.7M	8.9%	833K	9.1%	2.1M
Harrah's	NA	NA	8.6%	11.1M	8.2%	1.9M	7.9%	6.6M
Resorts Int.	NA	NA	10.7%	8.8M	10.6%	2.3M	9.2%	2.9M
Sands	NA	NA	9.4%	6.1M	8.1%	1.2M	7.6%	3.1M
Showboat	11.3%	880K	9.0%	15.2M	10.8%	1.7M	9.5%	8.0M
Tropicana	NA	NA	8.6%	10.5M	8.2%	2.3M	7.9%	5.4M
Trump Marina	63.3%	204K	9.7%	7.6M	8.7%	2.1M	7.4%	3.8M
Trump Plaza	10.5%	1.2M	8.6%	12.6M	8.7%	2.9M	8.5%	4.1M
Taj Mahal	11.1%	995K	10.3%	13.8M	9.2%	1.4M	7.8%	6M

NA=No machines of this denomination in the casino

CASINO	$5	WIN	$25	WIN/LOSS	$100	WIN	OTHER SLOTS	WIN/LOSS
Hilton	6.1%	789K	-2.0%	-135K	.04%	14K	58%	153K
Bally's	5.0%	1.4M	8.1%	190K	5.8%	62K	8.4%	747K
Caesars	7.2%	2.0M	5.2%	374K	2.9%	228K	3.2%	629K
Claridge	4.3%	234K	8.8%	59K	NA	NA	NA	NA
Harrah's	4.4%	1.6M	5.0%	138K	9.8%	209K	7.1%	699K
Resorts Int.	4.0%	596K	12.0%	117K	-15.4%	-52K	10.5%	128K
Sands	6.8%	1.1M	3.8%	62K	8.8%	44K	7.6%	331K
Showboat	4.8%	531K	33.2%	10K	89.9%	8K	5.4%	277K
Tropicana	2.0%	477K	6.4%	172K	7.6%	193K	5.3%	724K
Trump Marina	6.2%	839K	0.9%	52K	6.9%	263K	7.6%	409K
Trump Plaza	5.1%	100K	1.2%	47K	12.5%	204K	3.6%	197K
Taj Mahal	4.2%	1.5M	-1.6%	-97K	7.3%	127K	6.3%	323K

NA=No machines of this denomination in the casino

$100 machines, with Caesars netting the top $374,000 from their eleven machines. Two of the casinos were clobbered by the players, with a combined $232,000 loss.

The $5 machines were a modest winner for the casinos, with five of the twelve casinos taking in from $1.1 million to $2 million each, with the other seven netting only amounts in the hundreds of thousands.

When it came to the dollar machines, they all proved solid winners for the casinos, with an aggregate win of $55 million for the month. Only the gross on the quarter machines pulled in more revenue. Dollars easily outpaced the 50¢ machines, in some cases even yielding triple the income of the half-dollar slots.

The lowly nickel machine was no big earner for the casinos and, not coincidentally, five of the twelve casinos have discontinued them altogether.

When Atlantic City casinos first opened, it was obligatory by law to have 5¢ machines. Now, more than twenty years later, five casinos show no trace of a nickel slot. Revenue-wise these ceased to make sense, with just two casinos barely grossing a million each, and the others only hundreds of thousands.

The dime machine? It seems to have gone the way of the horse-and-buggy. Only one casino offered the 10¢ slots, that one being the World's Fair, which went belly-up in 1999.

The New Jersey Industry Report for April 1998 also broke down all the table games in the casinos, which we will cover now.

Table Game Statistics

As interesting as I found the information on the slots, the data on the table games was even more illuminating.

The report covered not only blackjack, craps, roulette, and baccarat, but also mini-baccarat and the Big Six Wheel. "Other games" encompassed Chinese games such as Pai Gow and Sic Bo as well as "Fast Action Hold 'Em" and Keno.

To my astonishment, the biggest percentage winner for the casino—in every casino—was the Big Six Wheel. The percentage of the win is so outrageously high that the casino owners should be arrested for thievery.

I always knew it was a rip-off, but only by reading the report did I discover just how much of a rip-off it is. Both the Sands and the Tropicana won more than fifty cents out of every dollar bet on that infernal Wheel! It was 52.9 percent and 50.9 percent respectively.

No casino had less than a 38.6 percent win, and ten of the twelve casinos netted better than 40 percent profit for the month.

Anyone who bets on the Big Six Wheel is a Class-A schmuck. Spread the word. Do your good deed for the day. The casino "fix" is in when it comes to the Big Six!

Though statistically you get a bigger bang for your buck at craps than at blackjack, seven of the twelve casinos showed a better take on craps, percentage-wise, than on blackjack.

Roulette is always a casino's gold mine, especially games with the double-zero wheel.

Baccarat is the fishnet for whales in all casinos. It is the big money game, and sometimes lucky players can damage the bottom line. Many of the big bettors are Asians, whom the casinos take great pains to accommodate in every way possible. It is not unusual for a whale to win or lose sums in the millions during his junket to a casino city.

Looking over the baccarat wins (and one loss) for the casinos in April, 1998, no pattern emerges. From the large 33.5 percent win for Harrah's—which amounted only to a small $35,774 in dollars—to the 6.0 percent loss for Trump Plaza—which translated into a big $157,041 loss in dollars—baccarat remains the wild card for the casino. And the win percentage has no relation to the

Percentage of Casino Winnings (or Losses)

CASINO	BLACKJACK	CRAPS	ROULETTE	BIG 6	BACC.	MINI BACC	OTHER GAMES
Hilton	10.5	12.7	22.5	46.4	7.9	12.3	18.0
Bally's	13.0	13.0	21.8	41.8	13.4	13.2	19.2
Caesars	14.4	9.1	18.9	43.8	10.3	7.1	21.1
Claridge	14.2	16.5	19.4	39.4	16.8	9.9	15.5
Harrah's	11.7	17.4	17.6	44.4	33.5	2.7	21.8
Resorts	11.5	14.4	23.4	44.0	18.5	16.4	16.7
Sands	17.6	12.4	25.9	52.9	21.5	16.5	22.4
Showboat	14.0	14.9	28.7	39.9	21.5	15.7	9.8
Tropicana	14.6	14.1	11.1	50.9	21.2	15.3	18.7
Trump Marina	14.6	22.9	27.9	38.6	11.8	-15.7	18.7
Trump Plaza	10.4	18.2	20.4	40.6	-6.0	13.6	20.7
Taj Mahal	13.9	12.4	24.3	42.5	7.0	20.9	22.9

amount earned or lost. The percentage refers only to the "drop." The Hilton, which had a very low 7.9 percent win, ended up with $384,000 in the till. Bally's 13.4 percent—almost double the Hilton's, yielded only $7,000 more in revenue.

Caesars, with a comparatively modest 10.3 percent, banked a cool $1.2 million. And the Taj, with the lowest percentage win of any of twelve casinos, ended up on top of the heap, with an impressive $1.65 million win for the month.

Mini-baccarat, is a comparatively new table game for some casinos. It showed some surprising statistics. Usually perceived in the crowded casino as just another table game on the floor, it doesn't have the aura of the baccarat pit. Yet to my astonishment, the figures show that mini-baccarat sometimes equals or even surpasses the grosses and losses of its big brother!

Three of the twelve casinos had bigger grosses on their mini-baccarat tables than on their regular baccarat tables. All three had more minis action than regular games.

The monthly baccarat grosses of the casinos were quite varied, from an impressive $2,642,000 high for the Taj, to a minuscule $59,000 for Harrah's (and that was the grand total for *both* baccarat games).

It is interesting to note that, although the Casino Control Commission has given its okay to fifteen "Other" games, most all of the casinos opt to run only five, usually three Chinese-oriented games, along with Caribbean and "Let-It-Ride" poker. The report also lists regular poker, which, for all its pop culture fame, only half the casinos offer. Of the ones that do, only the Taj had a take of more than a million for the month from that game.

The "Other Games" are also winners for the casinos, with percentages that run from a high of 22.9 for the Taj to a low of 9.8 for the Showboat. The Showboat was the only casino with a percentage win for "Other Games" that was lower than their win on both blackjack and craps.

Curiously, seven of the fifteen "Other Games" were shunned altogether by all the casinos, and four "Other Games" were offered in only five of the casinos.

Mini-craps was offered by three casinos, with win-percentages ranging from 7.5 percent to 22 percent. Mini-dice, a game separate from mini-craps, was offered only by the Taj, which reaped a fat 36.9 percent profit on it. "Fast Action Hold 'Em" was just at Harrah's, which netted a hefty 31.8 percent profit.

Keno, the last entry on the "Other Games" pages listed by the casinos, is a game heavily weighted percentage-wise in the casino's favor. Even though it has a better than 25-percent house edge, only six of the twelve casinos offered the game.

SCHEDULE OF CASINO WINS AND REVENUE FROM "OTHER GAMES"

TYPE OF GAME	AUTHORIZED UNITS	WIN/LOSS	DROP	WIN/LOSS PERCENTAGE
Sic Bo	2	$83,001	$267,610	31.0%
Pai Gow Poker	8	$651,354	$2,737,041	23.8%
Pai Gow	6	$636,104	$2,052,186	31.0%
Keno	10	$115,807	$396,070	29.2%
Caribbean Stud Poker	10	$591,314	$2,788,021	21.2%
Let It Ride Poker	7	$213,358	$1,847,562	11.5%
Mini-Dice	1	$55,312	$149,974	36.9%
TOTALS	44	$2,346,250	$10,238,464	22.9%

Gambling Around the Country

✓ Native American Casinos

✓ Waldorf, Maryland

✓ Vegas

✓ Atlantic City

✓ Mhoon Landing, Mississippi

✓ Gambling Ship, NYC

Native American Casinos

American Indian casinos are not bound by any Casino Commission rules. A few tribal casinos make public the percentage figures for the month, but most do not. Tribal lands are extraterritorial entities, recognized by treaties that go back to colonial days. The question of paying income and other federal taxes is moot.

The day-to-day regulation of a tribal casino is generally left to the tribal gaming authority, a situation that some have described as "the fox watching the hen house." Michigan tribal casinos all post signs that say the state doesn't regulate activities conducted within the confines of the casino.

♠ ♠ ♠ ♠ ♠

Most people don't realize that Minnesota has seventeen tribal casinos, almost a third more than Atlantic City. And all the casinos are within one hour's drive of each other or less.

♠ ♠ ♠ ♠ ♠

In a letter to the editor of a gambling magazine a senior citizen complained bitterly that Foxwoods in Connecticut has no nickel machines. "Are they greedy, or don't they care that older people on low incomes like to slow down the pace?"

"Foxwoods is so busy that it has neither the space nor the desire to offer nickel machines," was the curt, straightforward reply from the editor.

Waldorf, Maryland

Contrary to popular belief, prior to the arrival of casinos in Atlantic City in 1973, there was one locale in America, one oasis in the gambling-dry desert of the continental United States, where a thriving slot-machine metropolis was going strong, 24-hours-a-day, every day: Waldorf, Maryland.

Waldorf is but a dot on the map, a small locality on the highway that's less than an hour away from Washington, D.C. Here, during the 1950s and the late 60s, there were twenty busy slot machine palaces dotting the highway, strictly coin casinos with no table games, bearing familiar names such as The Golden Nugget and The Sands. How or why these came into existence, and why they were phased out by the early 70s is still unclear to me. But looking back on the scandal-ridden history of the politics of Maryland's state government at the time—one governor was removed from office, and former Maryland Governor Spiro Agnew had to resign the Vice Presidency under fire when it was proven that he was still getting payoffs from Maryland's shady enterprises even after he became Vice President—maybe it does add up. Besides, some of the proprietors of the Waldorf slot machine palaces looked like characters that stepped right out of Mario Puzo's *The Godfather*.

Whenever the annual American Booksellers Convention was held in Washington, D.C.—and for a period during the sixties it was anchored there—I'd make it my business to take at least one side trip to Waldorf, especially if I was attending the convention with a lady that I wanted to impress. One pretty miss who had never been in a casino—in fact, had never ever in her life even set eyes on a slot machine—was bowled over by the slot machine city. Trying her luck, she walked up to a four-quarter, double-barreled bandit, dropped in her six quarters, and spun the wheels for the first time in her life. Naturally, she hit the jackpot for $250.

Recently I was on a Greyhound bus going south and passed through Waldorf. No more slot machines, and no more crowds. Fun City was no more.

Vegas

Las Vegas's allure is irresistible to the world's tourists, and also for our country's conventioneers. *Tradeshow Week* magazine ranked Las Vegas at the top of their list of America's most popular convention sites in 1999. This oasis in the desert hosted 32 of the 200 largest conventions in the United States, followed distantly by Chicago and New York. But conventioneers beware! Las Vegas has its allure, and it also has its drawbacks. The noted Philadelphia attorney Albert B. Gerber booked a First Amendment Lawyers Association (FALA) annual meeting there. His endless problem was corralling FALA lawyers who were strung out at the gambling tables, and getting them into the seminars and meetings. Conventions in the following years were held in cities offering less razzle-dazzle.

All those genial, ever-smiling casino hosts and owners are always playing hardball, no matter how friendly they appear. Even when they go out of their way to comp you for a drink or a meal, they have only one thought in their mind, just one goal on their agendas: separating you from your money as quickly as possible. In case you doubt what I say, let me tell you about the gala opening day of Circus Circus in Las Vegas.

Ballyhooed for weeks prior to its debut as the first Las Vegas casino geared for the family crowd, opening day at Circus Circus was eagerly anticipated. When the day came, the crowds lined up early. Frankly, I didn't give a tinker's dam for a family-oriented casino as I was a foot-loose bachelor, and a casino was a casino, but this day I was with a lady friend-of-the-moment who was eager to see the new attraction. Reluctantly I said okay, and we joined the long line that snaked halfway to the next casino. I hadn't seen a line this long since the heyday of Radio City Music Hall. After an interminable wait we finally got inside. With all the hoopla and advance publicity, there was more razzle-dazzle than one could imagine. Bands, acrobats, circus animals. Dozens of carnival booths ringed the three-story building, with all the carnies hawking their wares and spieling their spiel, not to mention the jugglers, clowns, and trapeze artists that rounded out the pageant. You get the picture. The damn noise from all of the above was maddening. Fighting my way to a green-felt table—*any* green-felt table—was a hassle in itself. Finally I managed to squeeze in at a craps table (I really didn't want to shoot craps, but getting a seat at a blackjack table was well-nigh impossible). I stuck it out for a few hands because a guy at the other end of the table had a great shoot, but the cacophony was beginning to get to me. Able to stand it no longer, I picked up my chips and looked around for the cashier's cage. After wandering—and pushing—around for a few minutes I spotted a circus wagon frontage with the word "Paymaster" inscribed in ornate lettering. I must have been one of the first to cash in, as almost everyone else was preoccupied with the razzle-dazzle of opening day. I pushed my chips in to an impeccably dressed guy inside, one with a $2,000 suit and a $50 haircut. Saddled with a splitting headache from all the clamor, I just wanted out. "Just gimme my money and let me out of this bedlam. When I shoot

craps I sure as hell don't want to step into elephant shit! You better believe I'M NEVER COMING BACK TO THIS FUCKING
CRAZY CASINO AGAIN!"

Maybe I overreacted just a trifle, maybe I was rude to the dude,
but I just needed to express my desire to split as soon as possible.
Mad as a hatter, the guy, in all his sartorial splendor, counted out
my money, and gave me one of the dirtiest dirty looks I've ever been
zapped with, as I wheeled around and hightailed it out to the street.

A couple of weeks later in New York I picked up *Life* magazine
which, to my surprise, had an eight-page photo spread on the gala
opening of Circus Circus in Las Vegas. Along with all the pictures
was a short interview with the very same Beau Brummel from the
cashier's cage—Jay Sarno, one of the owners of Circus Circus.
"What makes me mad," he complained, "are these guys who come
in and hit and run and complain about elephant shit. We don't
have any elephants at Circus Circus."

Today, most casinos are corporate entities, run by MBA CEOs
with $1,000 suits, button-down shirts, and pricey ties. Their mar-
keting departments are jammed with high-tech computers and business machines manned by accountants that you would expect to
find in a shoelace factory's office. When I first got to Las Vegas in
the early 1960s, all the casinos were either controlled by the mob
or by free-wheeling, old-time gamblers who started out running
sawdust joints in the Old West. A lot of their accounting was done
in back rooms by shady-looking, cigarette-smoking characters wearing visors and wrinkled sport shirts.

Whenever a new casino would open, as the Castaways did in
the early 60s—an ill-fated venture built directly across from the
Sands—all the other High Rolling casino owners would swoop
down on opening day, loaded with money, and with the evil intent
to try their luck at the tables, doing their damnedest to put the
newcomer out of business. A wild idea to be sure, but a long-standing Vegas tradition nevertheless.

In the case of some new casinos, the ploy turned out to be an unexpected shot in the arm for the new kid on the block, and the old-timers retreated, licking their wounds. In the case of the Castaways, the good ol' boys had a lucky run at the tables and cleaned out the Castaways' cashier's cage by dawn. And damned if the casino wasn't forced to close its doors the very next day for a spell, until it was finally able to hustle up new financing for a reopening.

Atlantic City

Resorts was the first casino in Atlantic City in 1978. You stood in line to get in, and if you didn't have a jacket you were turned away at the door. Here's how the casino scene has changed in the first twenty years of legal gambling in Atlantic City:

> Annual Visitors
>   1978: 9.4 million
>   1998: 34.0 million
> Number of Slot Machines
>   1978: 893
>   1998: 34,539
> Number of Table Games
>   1978: 84
>   1998: 4,447

Mhoon Landing, Mississippi

While Las Vegas and Atlantic City casinos clawed at each other, fighting to entice patrons into their pleasure palaces, the Splash Casino in Mhoon Landing, Mississippi, opened in 1992, charging a $10-per-person entry fee! And would you believe that the local lollipops were standing on line to get in?

Gambling Ship, NYC

With great fanfare fueled by an expensive media blitz, the *Edinburgh Castle* set sail on Wednesday, January 28, 1998, from a West 55th Street pier in Manhattan. New York's first quasi-legal gambling ship was about to set sail. On board were hundreds of gamblers, all eager to get past the three-mile limit and into International waters so they could play blackjack, roulette, craps, and baccarat, and the two hundred slot machines on board. Each of the passengers paid $99 for the overnight cruise, the weekday price of admission. On weekend trips the cost doubled to $199 per person.

Just three months after launching, Manhattan Cruises threw in the towel. This ended the first legal high-seas gambling ship venture from the Big Apple.

The problem, according to President Mickey Brown, was that there just weren't that many gamblers who would pay $199, or even the $99 weekday rate. He complained that the almost three hundred workers on the ship sometimes outnumbered the paying customers.

The aborted effort of Manhattan Cruises didn't dampen the enthusiasm of other cruise companies. Five other companies have forked over the hefty $100,000 application fee to New York's Gambling Control Commission, and are awaiting the city's okay before launching their own gambling cruises from both Manhattan and Brooklyn.

Epilogue

✓ The Gambler Strikes Back, Parts II and III
✓ I Love This Game

The Gambler Strikes Back, Parts II and III

I had an enforced seven-month hiatus while I was recuperating from the traffic accident—then I returned to Atlantic City to see what changes had transpired during my absence.

There were changes all right. The casinos had added more neon and glitter, new and exotic slot machines, some imported from Australia and Europe and, to my chagrin, two of my best shots at the blackjack tables were done away with. Frankly, I wondered why it took both casinos that long to wise up.

Traditionally, I would make my first stop at Trump Plaza each and every trip, winning a hundred or two for my wife Stella, who waited patiently for me on a boardwalk bench. At times her "Mad Money" bank at home amounted to more than $3,000! My only ground rules for her spending were that it had to go for something expensive or something impractical, or both—on something she wouldn't ever spend her *own* money on. Definitely not for either toilet paper or a paint job for the kitchen. Once, unable to decide among ten chic Eric Javits hats she liked, she went wild with her Mad Money and bought 'em all!

Returning to my favorite blackjack pit at the Plaza, I was bitterly disappointed to see that the gaggle of $25-to-$5,000 tables had been downsized to Atlantic City's traditional $25-to-$1,000 ones. With the spread of $25 to the $5,000 limit I was able to live dangerously and nibble away at the table, green-chip-by-green-chip. Sure, through the years I had a few close calls as my bets

153

escalated perilously close to the five-grand limit, but I always stuck it out and many times left the table with at least a hundred or two hundred dollars of The Donald's money. And, yes, there were times he creamed me.

My other blackjack disappointment was at the Sands, where I'd always make a pit stop at their $25-to-$2,500 section. Maybe not as mathematically favorable as the Plaza, but I'd often have a hit-and-run success there, too. They too had eliminated the spread. Now it was $25 to $1,000. Resorts, on the other hand, juiced up their limits on the $25 tables to $3,000. New owners had taken over.

On the flip side of the Atlantic City odds, I was amused to see blackjack tables at Harrah's and Trump's Castle with limits of $50-to-$1000.

This spread is pure and simple thievery on the casino's part. The player has no chance.

Even though my two cornucopia pits had been done away with during my eight-month hiatus, I still rode the bus back to Manhattan with $2,300 of casino money. I just *had* to quit winners that Wednesday. If I didn't, I'd have no right to write this book.

It has now been more than three years since my spectacular back-to-back clean sweep of the Atlantic City casinos. On both trips I won in each and every casino and lost in none, prompting my publisher to commission me to write this book telling how I did it.

Now at last the book is completed and ready to turn in to the publisher. But before handing over my manuscript, I determined to return to Atlantic City still one more time, just to see if I could do it again.

On the first Wednesday in June I took the first (7:45 A.M.) bus, arriving at 10:30. In Park Place (the nearest casino to the new bus terminal) at 11:00, I made a pit stop at the casino cocktail lounge for a bracer, then headed directly over to the blackjack tables.

How did I do over-all? My score card, reproduced here, tells the story. I did have one close call at Resorts. After feasting on my obligatory King Crab claws, I left with less than my $200 goal, but managed to climb out of the $1,750 hole that I was in at one point.

Had I lost my seed money it would have been a very expensive seafood lunch. And at the Sands it was touch-and-go for more than an hour. Then I finally eked out a win and ran like a thief. As time was running out—I always plan on the 8:00 P.M. bus back to

My Return To The Casinos

Casino	Shoot for	Actual	Running Total
Park Place	200	+225	+225
Sands	200	+200	+425
Resorts	200	+150	+575
Taj Mahal	200	+575	+1,150
Showboat	200	+650	+1,800
Trump Plaza	200	+350	+2,150
Caesars	200	+450	+2,600
Park Place	200	+375	+2,975
Claridge	200	+275	+3,250
Hilton	200	+625	+3,875
Tropicana	200	+600	4,475
Trump Plaza	200	+100	+4,575
Caesars	200	+25	+4,600
Park Place	100	+50	+4,650

Manhattan—I prudently bypassed the two outlying casinos in the distant Marina, concentrating on the Boardwalk's ten casinos. I won at Park Place three times on the trip, compensating me for the two out-of-the-way casinos I bypassed. With less than an hour to make my bus, I won an extra twenty-five bucks at Caesars, and finally ducked into Park Place to win two green chips, which I put into my pocket and will use on my next trip to the seashore.

What was my final score card tally? I was in 14 casino forays and won 14 times.

So I did it again. But don't think I'm cocky and smugly self-assured over my sweep. Just the opposite. Each and every trip to a casino is a dramatic risk. Odds favor the casino, so if I'm not on guard constantly I know I'll go down the toilet. And as my old score cards reflected, there were days when I was wiped out, more days than I care to remember. My golden words of advice again: Hit and run. Nibble away. Never go for a big score in any one casino!

Frustrated, I noticed a couple of seats open at a $10-minimum table, so I thought what-the-hell, I only want to win a few bucks for a clean sweep score card, so I sat down and played a green chip on each of two spaces. To my delight, my first spot had a black-jack, and my second spot had a neat 19. With two great hands it didn't immediately dawn on me that the dealer had dealt his two cards *face-up*, showing a 19. He paid my blackjack, but only with even money. I told him I would, of course, stand on my 19, and then I bitterly learned the bitter truth about this particular table: It was a "Double-Exposure" blackjack table, with the words arcing —not very clearly—over the players' spots in the table middle. Except for those words, the layout was identical to all the other blackjack tables. Damn hard to notice, unless you're looking for it.

I learned that by "Double-Exposure" rules my 19 was loser against the dealer's 19! The only way I could win was to top the dealer's total, which meant *I had to hit my 19!* Sheer madness, but what could I do? I closed my eyes and hit, drawing a King of spades for a total of 29, the highest amount I ever drew in a blackjack hand.

The blackjack I had only paid even money, to compensate for the dealer's open hand. Happily my blackjack win canceled my Kamikazi hit on my 19, and everything evened out. I grabbed my two chips and ran to the cashier's cage, and then out the door.

My advice: Look before you play, and stay far away from "Double-Exposure" blackjack.

I Love This Game

After more than forty years of casino adventuring—and every casino visit has been an adventure—you might ask if I'm ahead of the game.

Early on in this book I promised to tell it like it is, and I have kept my word. Frankly, I cringe now when I think of some of my early stupidities in the casinos. The only reason I now dare to bare my shame is to warn you against doing what I did, and encourage you to do what I *should have* done.

I'll not dodge the question. The answer isn't a clear-cut yes or no.

At first I was a wide-eyed neophyte, overwhelmed by the razzle-dazzle of Las Vegas. My adventures were on a gambler's roller coaster—sometimes I'd come home with a score, too often I'd come back with just enough cash to pay my cab fare from the airport. I never took credit. What I lost, when I lost, was never rent money and definitely not any scared money. My seed money rarely exceeded $4,000—sometimes it was as much as five or six—and once foolishly $10,000 (it was a loser).

I'd cash $2,000 at a table, and keep the other thousands in my pocket. In the event that I hit a dry spell, I had the security of knowing that I had my reserve to fall back on. Occasionally I did win, and every now and then it was a goodie. After making my most memorable score of $31,125, I prudently invested most all of it in my mail-order book business; I made damn sure I didn't take it back with me to Las Vegas!

As I made more trips West I became a more savvy gambler. No longer did I make the usual dumb mistakes. No longer did I depend on the slot machines to make my fortune. Gone was my obsession with beating Keno.

No longer did I make a foolhardy shot for the moon, and I didn't try to make a big score in any one casino. Smaller, more realistic payouts were now my goal, done carefully casino-by-casino.

Blackjack became my game of choice. Sure, baccarat had slightly better odds as did craps, but I found that I was more comfortable at blackjack, and the illusion that I had more control over the action.

And there is yet *another* dimension to the equation. Outside of the monetary winnings and losings I've experienced in my almost half-century of casino adventuring, there was the flavorsome lifestyle that accompanied it all, this during the most important years of my life. Perhaps I was most influenced by my long-time mentor, friend, and publisher, Lyle Stuart, who had—and still has—a James Bond way-of-life. He was the one who prodded me to fly all the way out to Las Vegas in 1960 for my first brief weekend stay, just to see a casino floor show: Frank Sinatra, Dean Martin, Sammy Davis, Jr., and Peter Lawford—the Rat Pack cavorting at the Sands.

The memory of that first trip and that first show is one of the fondest and most cherished of my life. There and then I was introduced to the casino—a fantasy world of glitter and gold. I've now spent almost a half-a-century "commuting" to Pleasure Island and enjoying most of it! (I use the term Pleasure Island as a symbolic name for *all* the casinos around the world that I have adventured in during a lifetime.)

For me, it has been a lot better than spending almost five decades of my life going fishing and watching TV in East Cupcake, Iowa. (My apologies to everyone living in East Cupcake. I'm sure you're happy there, but it just isn't my idea of fun.)

It's comforting for me to know that if ever I'm in a rut in Manhattan, at loose ends with myself, an adventure surely awaits me only two-hours away in Atlantic City, not to mention all those mouth-watering King Crab claws.

Appendix

✓ The Worst Bets for the Player
✓ Portrait of the Hit-and-Runner: My Score Cards

The Worst Bets for the Player

Here is a breakdown of some of the Best Bets in the casino—Best Bets *for* the casino. Worst bets for the player, as printed in *The High Roller*.

SOME OF THE BIGGEST PAYOFFS AT TABLE GAMES
1000-to-one: Royal flush at Let It Ride.
200-to-one: Straight flush at Let It Ride.
100-to-one: Royal flush at Caribbean Stud.
60-to-one: 4 or 17 in Sic Bo.
50-to-one: Straight flush at Caribbean Stud.
50-to-one: Four-of-a-kind at Let It Ride.
45-to-one: Joker and casino symbol on Big Wheel.
35-to-one: Inside number at Roulette.
30-to-one: 2 or 12 in Craps.
20-to-one: Four-of-a-kind at Caribbean Stud.
18-to-one: 5 or 16 at Sic Bo.
15-to-one: 3 or 11 in craps.

Like a newspaper listing contaminated beaches, and the Health Department listing the restaurants with serious cleanliness problems, I have listed these twelve worst bets for the player so as to warn you to avoid these wagers. Sure, BIG payoffs if you win—but the problem here is that it's a rather small chance for you to win.

Save your casino bankroll for betting on propositions that will give you at least a fighting chance to go home with some of the casino's money!

Portrait of the Hit and Runner: My Score Cards

Whenever I remembered to, I saved my score cards. They are the immortalized records of my forays into the casinos of Nevada and Atlantic City. When I'd come home from a session, I'd either toss the card into a drawer or drop it on my desk. Eventually, when I tidied up, often it would find its way into the wastebasket. Only now that I've been commissioned to write this book on gambling have I finally rummaged through the drawer to see exactly what I had saved.

Sorting the hundreds of score cards and carefully laying them out on the kitchen table was a traumatic experience for me. Seeing them as a cohesive entity was both awesome and instructive. Frankly, I just couldn't believe that I gambled in so many casinos in over forty years. And I was looking at only *some* of my forays! Now I'm sorry I didn't save every blessed one of them.

Because I didn't foresee ever using them for a book, I didn't bother to date the cards. I can pinpoint a few cards timewise by the information on the casino promotion piece, the back of which I had used as a makeshift score card. I did date a couple, but damned if I remember today why I went out of my way to do it.

Going through my piles of cards, I chose unusual ones—some winners, some losers.

Once Atlantic City opened up, my flights to Las Vegas became fewer. Puerto Rico casinos were the pits; I loved the country but hated their casinos. The limits were low, guaranteed to grind down the player, and as the rules were rigged in the casino's favor. I have never met anyone who ever won money in the Puerto Rico casinos. I only bet in Puerto Rico to make drink or dinner money. And my betting limit was always 25 bucks, tops.

I'm offering a representative selection from my score cards because I believe you can learn from them, not only what to do, but more importantly what *not* to do. You'll see that sometimes I did make a score but, greedy schmuck that I was, I foolishly stayed around too long and eventually pissed it all away. Happily, some score cards show my gambling acumen, as I took my winnings and ran right out of the casino and hurried home on the next plane or bus. I hope when you win you'll also take the cash and run like hell.

Portrait of the Hit-and-Runner: My Score Cards

How to Win $25,000...

Casino	Shoot For	Actual	Running Total
Sahara	1000	+1000	+1000
Int'l	1000	+1000	+2000
Landmark	500	+500	+2500
Sands	500	+1000	+3500
Riviera	500	-3000	+500
Riviera	500	+1900	+2400
Riviera	500	+2000	+4400
Bonanza	500	+600	+5000
Dunes	500	+900	+5900
Sahara	1000	+3600	+9500
Sahara	500	+1500	+11000
Dunes	500	+1500	+12500
CP	100	-10600	+1900
CP	500	+1200	+3100
CP	500	+1700	+4800
CP	200	+300	+5100
CP	900	+900	+6000
T-Bird	1000	+1200	+7200
T-Bird	1000	+1600	+8600
CP	1000	+6200	+14800
CP	200	+300	+15100
Trop	500	+5500	+20600
Aladdin	500	+2800	+23400
Bonanza	500	+3200	+26600
Dunes	500	+3700	+30300
Sahara	500	+1700	+32000
Sahara	500	+2200	+34200
Sahara	1000	+3800	+38000
Sahara	1000	-15200	+22800
Trop	2000	+2300	+25100

And How to Lose $25,000.

Casino	Shoot For	Actual	Running Total
T's Castle	300	-1625	-1625
Showboat	300	+875	-750
Taj	300	-2150	-2900
Resorts	500	-1900	-4800
Sands	500	0	-4800
T Plaza	500	-2500	-7300
Caesars	1000	0	-7300
T Plaza	1000	-1625	-8920
Caesars	1000	-3075	-12000
Park Place	500	-1700	-13700
Claridge	500	+1700	-12000
Showboat	300	+925	-11025
Hilton	500	-3625	-14650
Hilton	300	+475	-14175
Sands	500	-4675	-18850
P. Place	5000	-6000	-24850

A Day I Could Do Nothing Wrong...

Casino	Shoot For	Actual	Running Total
Gold Nug.	100	+70	+70
Horseshoe	100	+50	+120
Sahara	100	+70	+190
T-Bird	100	+30	+220
Riviera	100	+40	+260
Circ., Circ.	100	+50	+310
D. I.	100	+60	+370
Sands	100	+110	+480
Caesars	100	+50	+530
Aladdin	100	+100	+630
Dunes	100	+130	+760
MGM	100	+150	+910
Trop.	100	+130	+1040

Except For The Dunes, A Day I Could Do Nothing Right...

Casino	Shoot For	Actual	Running Total
Trop	100	-575	-575
Aladdin	200	-1290	-1865
Aladdin	2000	-500	-2360
Dunes	1000	+1300	-1065
Dunes	300	+165	-900
Sands	200	-600	-1500
Castaway	200	-275	-1775
Aladdin	200	-475	-2250

Two Prime Examples Of How You Can Whittle Away At The Casinos:

Casino	Shoot For	Actual	Running Total
Int'l	50	+100	+100
Landmark	50	+30	+130
Sands	50	+10	+140
Riviera	50	+30	+170
Dunes	30	+30	+200
Sahara	20	+20	+220
Dunes	25	+25	+245
CP	15	+15	+260
T-Bird	60	+60	+320
CP	15	+15	+335
Trop	15	+22	+367
Aladdin	50	+93	+460
L. Ceasars	1	+3.35	+463.35
Bonanza	20	+20	+483.35
Dunes	15	+25	508.35
Sahara	15	+15	+523.35
Sahara	25	+25	+548.35

Casino	Shoot For	Actual	Running Total
Trop	50	+60	+60
Paradise	50	+30	+90
Marina	50	+40	+130
Aladdin	50	-70	+60
Sahara	100	+50	+110
Riviera	100	+55	+165
Frontier	100	+15	180
DI	100	-60	+120
Sands	100	+50	+170
Castaway	50	+30	+200
Dunes	100	+70	+270
CP	100	+75	+345
MGM	100	+60	+405
Dunes	100	+110	+515
CP	100	-110	+405
CP	150	+60	+465
G. Nugget	100	-60	+405
Horsesho	100	+70	+475
4-Queens	100	+15	+490
MGM	100	+110	+600
Dunes	100	+105	+705
MGM	100	-115	+590
MGM	100	+130	+720
MGM	100	-70	+650